CONSTRUCTING PURCHASING POWER PARITIES USING A REDUCED INFORMATION APPROACH

A RESEARCH STUDY

JANUARY 2021

ASIAN DEVELOPMENT BANK

ADB

Notes:
In this publication, "$" refers to United States dollars, unless otherwise stated.

Cover design by Rhommell Rico.

Cover photos by Eric Sales and Jawad Jalali for ADB.
Far Left: Students attentively watch their teacher's presentation at a high school in Mongolia.
Inside Left: A woman prepares fabric for sale at a textile shop in Bhutan.
Inside Right: A purchase is made at the Mandave market in Kabul, Afghanistan.
Far Right: Fresh foods on display at the Gum Market in Yerevan, Armenia.

Contents

Tables and Figures

Foreword

Since the turn of the millennium, there has been increasing use of purchasing power parities (PPPs) and PPP-based gross domestic product data, produced under the International Comparison Program (ICP), for economic and statistical analysis. This includes the use of PPPs in calculating indicators that help monitoring some of the critical goals and targets of the Sustainable Development Goals.

The ICP is, however, a highly complex global program that demands significant allocation of human and financial resources and years of careful planning in implementing price-collection surveys.

Because of the immense resources needed for data collection and project management during an ICP benchmark year, ICP cycles have not been conducted frequently and PPPs for nonbenchmark years have been conventionally estimated using simple extrapolation techniques. However, when there are long intervals between ICP cycles, this methodology yields estimates that are inconsistent with the benchmark figures. The wide differences between the extrapolated PPPs and the actual benchmarks for the ICP's 2005 and 2011 cycles led to considerable debate among statisticians and development practitioners. The Asian Development Bank (ADB) has therefore undertaken methodological research initiatives to find cost-effective alternative approaches to PPP estimation during nonbenchmark years. The "core list" approach was developed in ADB's 2009 research study, *2009 Purchasing Power Parity Update for Selected Economies in Asia and the Pacific* (ADB 2012a).

A second similar study for 2016 was conceptualized after the release of the results of the ICP's 2011 cycle and before the 2017 cycle was announced, to validate the methodologies developed in 2009. The study aimed to assess the use of 2016 prices from capital cities of a reduced or "core" product list, to produce accurate estimates as though a full-scale ICP cycle had been implemented in that year. It should, however, be noted that, while price collection for this research study was in progress, simultaneous preparations for the ICP's 2017 cycle also needed to be initiated—pursuant to the recommendations of the United Nations Statistical Commission in March 2016. Given the importance of the 2017 cycle, and to follow the global schedule for its completion, work on the full-scale ICP benchmark was prioritized and finalization of the research report on the 2016 data was deferred until the main 2017 ICP reports were completed and released, which occurred in October 2020.

With the analytical work on the 2016 data now undertaken, this report presents the methodology and estimates of 2016 PPPs for the currencies of the 20 participating economies, price levels, and real (PPP-converted) gross domestic product and its major components. This analysis takes into account individual consumption expenditure by households, government final consumption expenditure, gross fixed capital formation, changes in inventories and acquisitions less disposals of valuables, and balance of exports and imports.

By contributing to the efforts to develop alternative and cost-effective methods of estimating PPPs for nonbenchmark years of the ICP, this research study will guide the Asia and Pacific region as it moves to implement a 3-year ICP cycle, following recommendations of the United Nations Statistical Commission, before eventually moving to the generation of annual PPPs.

There are, of course, many people who have devoted countless hours to the successful completion of this project. I wish to express my sincere appreciation and thanks to the World Bank ICP Global Office for the technical assistance in shaping the methodology in the early stages of the study; the dedicated ICP team of ADB's Statistics and Data Innovation Unit; other individual experts associated with the study; and, most importantly, the implementing agencies in the 20 participating economies. Without the dedicated efforts of these implementing agencies in conducting the prices surveys and compiling the national accounts estimates needed, this research program would not have been successful.

Yasuyuki Sawada
Chief Economist and Director General
Economic Research and Regional Cooperation Department
Asian Development Bank

Acknowledgments

This research study on 2016 purchasing power parities (PPPs) was carried out under the International Comparison Program (ICP) for Asia and the Pacific and was implemented by the Statistics and Data Innovation Unit of the Economic Research and Regional Cooperation Department of the Asian Development Bank (ADB).

The ICP team at ADB worked closely with the implementing agencies of the 20 participating economies in conducting the price surveys, and during validation of prices and national accounts, in order to compile the data needed for the research study. Special thanks to the heads of implementing agencies, designated ICP national coordinators, deputy national coordinators, and the ICP teams in the 20 participating economies for their cooperation, dedication, and hard work in collecting and validating the data needed for the study: Bangladesh Bureau of Statistics, Bangladesh; National Statistics Bureau, Bhutan; Department of Economic Planning and Statistics, Brunei Darussalam; National Institute of Statistics, Cambodia; Fiji Bureau of Statistics, Fiji; Census and Statistics Department, Hong Kong, China; Ministry of Statistics and Programme Implementation, India; Badan Pusat Statistik, Indonesia; Lao Statistics Bureau, Lao People's Democratic Republic; Department of Statistics, Malaysia; National Bureau of Statistics, Maldives; National Statistics Office of Mongolia, Mongolia; Central Bureau of Statistics, Nepal; Pakistan Bureau of Statistics, Pakistan; Philippine Statistics Authority, Philippines; Department of Statistics, Singapore; Department of Census and Statistics, Sri Lanka; Directorate-General of Budget, Accounting, and Statistics, Taipei,China; Trade Policy and Strategy Office, Thailand; and General Statistics Office, Viet Nam.

Sincere appreciation goes to the World Bank ICP Global Office for technical assistance through valuable contributions of Yuri Dikhanov in the early stages of this project, especially for the overall methodology of the study based on the core list approach and for selection of the core product lists and inputs during the regional data validation workshops. Sincere appreciation also goes to D. S. Prasada Rao for his regular advice and guidance in the finalization of the research study.

Kaushal Joshi, ADB principal statistician and the regional coordinator of the ICP for Asia and the Pacific, led the project, and was supported by Eileen Capilit and Arturo Martinez Jr. in the early stages of data collection and validation. Criselda de Dios, ADB economics and statistics analyst, provided technical and coordination support. National consultants, namely, Mel Lorenzo Accad, Paolo Kris Adriano, Rhea-Ann Bautista, Juan Miguel dela Cruz, Virginia Ganac, Mario Ilagan II, and Eleanore Ramos undertook extensive data validation, data analysis for calculation of results, and preparation of tabulations and charts in this research report.

D. S. Prasada Rao and Kaushal Joshi led the analysis of the results and the writing of this report, with the research supported by project team members. Maria Roselia Babalo, Oth Marulou Gagni, and Aileen Gatson provided administrative support. Paul Dent edited the manuscript, while Rhommell Rico created the cover design, and Joseph Manglicmot undertook typesetting of the report. Finally, the publishing team in ADB's Department of Communications provided guidance on production issues, performed overall compliance checks, and assisted in web dissemination. The Logistics Management Unit of the Office of Administrative Services facilitated the timely printing of the publication.

Elaine S. Tan
Advisor, Office of the Chief Economist and Director General
and Head, Statistics and Data Innovation Unit

Abbreviations

ADB	Asian Development Bank
AICH	actual individual consumption by households
CCEG	collective consumption expenditure by government
CPD	country-product-dummy
CPI	consumer price index
ECOSOC	United Nations Economic and Social Council
GCF	gross capital formation
GDP	gross domestic product
GEKS	Gini-Éltető-Köves-Szulc
GFCE	government final consumption expenditure
GFCF	gross fixed capital formation
HK$	Hong Kong dollar
ICEG	individual consumption expenditure by government
ICEH	individual consumption expenditure by households
ICP	International Comparison Program
IMF	International Monetary Fund
LCU	local currency unit
NPISHs	nonprofit institutions serving households
NSO	national statistics office
PLI	price level index
PPP	purchasing power parity
SNA	System of National Accounts
SPD	structured product description
UNSC	United Nations Statistical Commission

1. Introduction

Comparing macroeconomic measures, such as gross domestic product (GDP) or GDP per capita, between economies should be approached with caution. Such comparisons require conversion of national accounts aggregates, which are generally available in the local currency unit of each economy, to a common currency. This is often achieved by converting an economy's GDP into United States (US) dollars via the economy's US dollar exchange rate. An exchange rate is the number of units of an economy's currency that are required to purchase one unit of another economy's currency (e.g. $1) and thus reflects the "price" of a foreign currency. Exchange rates are appropriate currency converters to be used for many intereconomy comparisons. They are, for example, appropriate conversion factors for calculating the value of an economy's exports, to determine what could be imported with a particular level of exports, or for calculating the economy's balance of payments or foreign direct investments. However, when comparing GDP or GDP per capita across economies, or contrasting related macroeconomic aggregates and productivity levels, the use of exchange rates has been widely considered inadequate for several reasons. Since exchange rates can be affected by a range of nonmonetary factors that influence the demand for and supply of currencies, there potentially can be volatility in exchange rate movements. Another limitation in using exchange rates is that they do not reflect differences in price levels across economies. Most exchange rates generally overstate prices in developing economies, and consequently understate the volume of goods and services produced in developing economies.

The limitations of exchange rates in comparing standards of living between economies led to the research and development of meaningful alternative currency conversion factors or purchasing power parities (PPPs). These conversion factors are not based only on internationally traded goods and services, but also account for the prices of all nontraded goods and services included in GDP aggregates. Such nontraded goods and services are generally cheaper in low-wage economies than might be otherwise implied when using exchange rates to convert their values to a common currency. Thus, PPPs are designed to adjust for exchange rates as well as for differences in internal price levels between economies. Hence, comparisons of standards of living across economies are better achieved by comparing the volumes of goods and services that are actually available to the residents of each economy and calculated by using PPPs as conversion factors.

The International Comparison Program: Origins and Developments

The need for a meaningful alternative to exchange rates led to the pioneering work of Gilbert and Kravis (1954) and Gilbert and Associates (1958). Their work revealed some considerable differences between the exchange rates and the PPPs, especially for the developing economies, reflecting the differences in relative price levels across economies. This research and its associated findings finally led to the establishment of the International Comparison Program (ICP), which began in 1968 as a small-scale research project at the University of Pennsylvania, led by professors Kravis, Heston, and Summers. Since then, the program has grown steadily in terms of methods used, participation of economies, and program governance, to the point that it is now recognized as a global statistical initiative (ADB 2020). The status of the ICP can be measured by the fact that, for the most recent benchmark year of 2017, 176 economies from around the world participated in the program.

The ICP is a collaborative statistical work program with global coverage. It is undertaken under the guidance of the United Nations Statistical Commission (UNSC), with the principal objective of providing internationally comparable macroeconomic data on GDP and its components, PPPs of currencies, and price levels. The ICP Global Office, which is located at the headquarters of the World Bank, coordinates the program with active cooperation and assistance from the regional implementing agencies, which manage the comparisons in their respective regions. The regional implementing agencies are the African Development Bank; the Asian Development Bank (ADB); the Interstate Statistical Committee of the Commonwealth of Independent States; the Organisation for Economic Co-operation and Development; the Statistical Office of the European Communities; the United Nations Economic and Social Commission for Western Asia; and the United Nations Economic Commission for Latin America.

Since its inception, the ICP has been conducted for irregular benchmark years: 1970, 1975, 1980, 1985, 1993, 2005, 2011, and 2017. This has resulted in an increasing demand from stakeholders to make PPPs available in a more frequent, timely, and consistent manner. Accordingly, the UNSC, during its 47th session held in March 2016, endorsed the ICP to become a permanent element of its global statistical work program. The UNSC endorsed a shortened interval between ICP benchmark cycles—as advocated by the Friends of the Chair Group in its final evaluation of the ICP's 2011 cycle (ECOSOC 2016a)—recommending that benchmark cycles beyond 2017 be conducted every 3 years (ECOSOC 2016b).

ADB's Role in Advancing the International Comparison Program

Since 2005, ADB has taken the lead role as the regional implementing agency for the ICP in Asia and the Pacific. At the time of this report, the bank had successfully completed the ICP's cycles for 2005, 2011, and 2017, releasing the final report for the 2017 cycle in October 2020 (ADB 2020).

Through ADB's involvement, the ICP in the Asia and Pacific region has served as a knowledge-building exercise, generating invaluable experience for the program team within ADB and for ICP coordinators in participating economies. In the process, the program has led to enhanced capacity within national statistics offices on internationally comparable standards and methods, as well as their application to the official statistics produced by such offices. A great degree of knowledge transfer has been achieved through a series of technical workshops conducted from 2005 to 2020. To ensure enthusiastic participation by the region's economies, who are the main stakeholders of the program, the ICP in Asia and the Pacific has been run successfully by creating a spirit of cooperation and a sense of ownership of the program among the economies.

Implementation of the ICP—and compilation of internationally comparable price and volume measures of GDP and its expenditure components—is both complex and challenging. Undertaking intereconomy comparisons in Asia and the Pacific is a formidable task, given the socioeconomic diversity of the region and the variance in size of the economies included in the comparisons. Asia and the Pacific is home to some of the fastest-growing economies in the world, along with some transition economies such as Cambodia, the Lao People's Democratic Republic, and Viet Nam. The region also exhibits considerable disparities in levels of development, standards of living, and consumption patterns. The People's Republic of China and India, for instance, are two of the world's most populous countries and also two of its largest economies (World Bank 2015; World Bank 2020), while Singapore and Hong Kong, China are two economies with relatively small populations despite being among the richest economies in terms of real income per capita. At the same time, the Asia and Pacific region also includes small-island economies with very small populations, such as Fiji and Maldives, with limited economic capacity.

This regional complexity and diversity presented serious measurement and operational issues that had to be resolved during the implementation of the past three ICP cycles: 2005, 2011, and 2017. Consequently, ADB, in its role as the regional implementing agency, had to find innovative and practical solutions to these issues.

To illustrate the point, during the ICP's 2005 cycle, comparisons of wages and salaries of government employees across economies posed serious challenges. This was because data provided by some economies showed significantly low salaries for government employees, resulting in estimated PPPs that were quite low and, consequently, leading to implausibly high levels of real government expenditure in these economies. It was recognized that the low salaries of government employees in some economies might reflect low labor productivity in the government sector. As a solution, a method was devised and implemented to adjust for differences in productivity levels across economies during the 2005 cycle (ADB 2007). Until that time, the notion of productivity adjustment was not common within the ICP framework. ADB introduced a critical innovation that, in various forms refined over the ICP's 2011 and 2017 cycles, is now implemented in other regions facing similar issues, and also by the ICP Global Office in its global linking procedures. A refined procedure articulated in Inklaar (2019) was used to adjust the data collected in the 2017 cycle.

Another important contribution of ADB to the ICP agenda is the bank's effort to compile meaningful and plausible estimates of price levels and real expenditures for dwelling services. The two standard ICP methods—the rental price and quantity indicator approaches—did not work well when implemented for Asia and the Pacific in 2005 and 2011. Despite serious efforts in collecting reliable data on housing rents, along with quantity and quality indicators, the resulting price and volume comparisons remained highly implausible. To resolve this, ADB proposed and implemented the "reference volume approach" during the ICP's 2005, 2011, and 2017 cycles. The most progress on methodology was made during the 2017 cycle, when a new quality-adjusted, mixed rental-quantity indicator approach was developed, tested, and presented to the Technical Advisory Group of the ICP. The new approach proposed by ADB was acknowledged as a major breakthrough and it has been recommended that, after further testing, the new method should be implemented during the ICP's next cycle.

ADB recognizes the importance of accurate national accounts data as inputs to PPP calculations. It has devoted considerable resources and efforts since 2005 to build capacity for the compilation of national accounts data within the participating economies of Asia and the Pacific. The bank has also implemented two major projects on the construction of supply and use tables—initiatives that have enabled more than 18 economies in the region to compile these tables, leading to improved compliance with the United Nations System of National Accounts (ADB 2012b; ADB 2017).

In addition to developing improved methodologies, ADB has undertaken some innovative research projects related to the ICP, and two of them deserve special mention.

The first was a research project focusing on poverty-specific PPPs for the measurement of regional and global poverty thresholds and incidence, with the findings published in 2008 (ADB 2008). This project highlighted the need to conduct special surveys to collect the prices of goods and services that constitute the consumption baskets of the poor, and to focus on the types of outlets where the poor mostly fulfill their consumption needs. The project concluded that only replacing the national accounts expenditure shares with the expenditure weights of poor households from household surveys, while still using the price data from the ICP, was of limited importance in calculating poverty PPPs.

The other project of direct relevance to this report is a research study to identify suitable methodologies for updating the PPPs for 2005 to the year 2009, without the need to conduct extensive price surveys as undertaken for the ICP's benchmark years. The method based on the "reduced information approach" generated estimates of PPPs and real expenditures for 2009 and these were presented in an ADB research publication in 2012 (ADB 2012a).

About This Research Study: Motivations and Objectives

The ICP is a highly complex program requiring extensive coordination between the ICP Global Office at the World Bank, the regional implementing agency at ADB, and the implementing agencies in the participating economies. The program demands significant allocation of human and financial resources by all agencies at all levels. Implementation of each ICP cycle requires years of careful planning on the preparation of lists of goods and services to be priced by the economies; the design and execution of specific surveys to collect price data in each of the participating economies; rigorous data validation prior to the actual compilation; and, finally, the calculation of PPPs, price level indexes, and real expenditures at the GDP level as well as at the level of GDP components.

Given such huge resource requirements for the data collection and management of ICP operations, it is unsurprising that ICP cycles have not been conducted at more frequent intervals. The four most

recent cycles were conducted in the benchmark years of 1993, 2005, 2011, and 2017. To meet the demand for PPPs between benchmark years, extrapolation techniques are used by the World Bank to estimate PPPs for GDP and household consumption expenditure, and these are published in *World Development Indicators*, the World Bank's compilation of internationally comparable statistics on global development. However, extrapolating PPPs is problematic when there are long periods between benchmark cycles, with wide divergences often observed between the benchmark results and the extrapolations. The size of divergence and systematic patterns seen when comparing extrapolations with the actual results from the ICP's 2005 and 2011 cycles led to considerable debate and discussion among statisticians and development practitioners (Deaton and Aten 2017).

Comparability problems can also arise due to methodological changes from one ICP cycle to the next. Minimizing these issues requires either more frequent ICP benchmark cycles and a relatively consistent methodology for generating PPPs, or the development of innovative methods that are not resource intensive and can provide comparable and reliable PPPs between benchmark years. It should be noted that the demand for more frequent compilation of ICP results has been recognized by the Statistical Office of the European Communities, which produces comparisons for its economies on an annual basis, and by the Organisation for Economic Co-operation and Development, which produces PPPs every 3 years.

Of course, increasing the frequency of ICP cycles would incur costs that may be too high for many participating economies and regional implementing agencies. It is therefore necessary to balance the frequency of the ICP's cycles with alternative approaches that can reduce implementation costs and resource requirements while delivering reliable approximations of the PPPs and real expenditures garnered from each full-scale ICP cycle.

With these alternative approaches in mind, ADB implemented a research study to update the ICP's 2005 results by estimating PPPs for 2009. The outcomes of this 2009 study were published in 2012 (ADB 2012a). The study collected prices for a reduced list of products derived from the ICP's 2005 benchmark product lists. Additionally, prices were collected only in capital cities (then adjusted to national averages based on the relationships observed in the ICP's 2005 data). This approach considerably reduced the burden of data collection and data processing operations. However, the researchers concluded that, while the approach was satisfactory for interim years, it may not be suitable for a full benchmark cycle because relationships between capital-city prices and those for the rest of the economy are unlikely to remain stable over long periods of time.

To further examine and, if possible, refine the reduced information approach used in the 2009 study, ADB commissioned the research detailed in this report. After the successful completion of the ICP's 2011 cycle and publication of the associated report (ADB 2014), ADB began preparations for updating the 2011 PPPs for Asia and the Pacific to the interim year 2016. Similar to the 2009 study, the main objective of the research project was to implement a survey framework that reduces resource requirements and cost burden for participating economies, while yielding reliable PPP estimates.

All 23 economies involved in the ICP's 2011 cycle were invited to participate in the interim project, and 20 economies agreed to take part. The participating economies were: Bangladesh; Bhutan; Brunei Darussalam; Cambodia; Fiji; Hong Kong, China; India; Indonesia; the Lao People's Democratic Republic; Malaysia; Maldives; Mongolia; Nepal; Pakistan; the Philippines; Singapore; Sri Lanka; Taipei,China; Thailand; and Viet Nam. The People's Republic of China; Macau, China; and Myanmar were the three economies that were part of the ICP's 2011 benchmark cycle, but not part of the 2016 research study.

It should be noted that, while the price collection surveys for the 2016 research study were in progress, simultaneous preparations for the ICP's 2017 cycle had to be initiated by all participating economies and by ADB as the regional implementing agency. Considering the importance of the benchmark cycle, it was given priority of resources. Although collection and validation of the 2016 data continued, finalization of the research report was postponed until the completion and release of the two reports of the 2017 ICP cycle, which occurred in May and October 2020.

Structure of the Report

This report presents the results of a methodology based on a reduced price information. It reports the estimates of PPPs and other indicators for 2016 in respect of 20 participating economies from across Asia and the Pacific. Chapter 2 offers some explanations of basic concepts and discusses selected measures emanating from the ICP and multilateral comparisons. Chapter 3 presents the general framework and methodology of the ICP and reviews a few alternative approaches to the ICP, including those based on reduced information approaches. Chapter 4 describes the reduced information approach that was proposed and implemented in this research project. Chapter 5 presents the estimates of PPPs and real expenditures from this study. Finally, Chapter 6 offers conclusions from the research project and discusses the way forward for reduced information methods in the current context where ICP is to be implemented every three years.

2. Basic Concepts and Key Measures of the International Comparison Program

The central objective of the International Comparison Program (ICP) is to provide internationally comparable measures of economic activity in economies around the world. Expenditures on gross domestic product (GDP) and its components form the basis for international comparisons within the ICP. However, because measures such as GDP are specific to the economy in which they are observed, they are usually expressed in local currency units. The next step is therefore to identify and estimate suitable currency converters that can be used to convert economy-specific measures into internationally comparable aggregates. Exchange rates are often used to convert GDP for comparisons across economies, but these rates do not account for different price levels in each economy. In contrast, purchasing power parities (PPPs) generated from the ICP reflect the prices paid for acquiring goods and services in each economy participating in the program and are therefore better suited for intereconomy comparisons of standards of living.

Basic Concepts

The following are some key concepts that underpin the ICP. In-depth discussion of these measures is available within the main report on the ICP's 2017 cycle in Asia and the Pacific, which was released in October 2020 (ADB 2020).

Purchasing Power Parities

The first and most central measure for the ICP is the purchasing power parity (PPP) of a currency. PPP is a measure of the prices of goods and services in a given economy, relative to the prices for the same goods and services in a reference economy. For example,

when making comparisons between economies in Asia and the Pacific, the reference economy selected is Hong Kong, China and the reference currency used is the Hong Kong dollar (HK\$). Suppose a basket of goods and services representing consumption by households can be purchased for HK\$100 in Hong Kong, China. If the same basket of goods and services can be purchased for 600 Pakistan rupees (PRe) in Pakistan, then the PPP between Hong Kong dollars and Pakistan rupees is HK\$1.00 = PRe6.00.

The System of National Accounts 2008 defines the PPP of economy B with reference to economy A as "the number of units of B's currency that are needed in B to purchase the same quantity of individual good or service as one unit of A's currency will purchase in A" (United Nations 2009, para. 15.199). In other words, PPP is a spatial price deflator and currency converter that eliminates the effects of price level differences between economies, allowing volume comparisons of GDP and its components.

Some important aspects of this concept are:

- PPP is always measured relative to a reference economy (also referred to as the base economy).
- The currency of the reference economy is referred in economics parlance as the "numeraire currency". In the above example, Hong Kong, China is the reference economy and the Hong Kong dollar is the numeraire or reference currency.
- PPP is always measured with respect to a basket of goods and services, and therefore can be different for different baskets of goods and services. As a result, PPPs are calculated for specific expenditure groups such as household consumption expenditure, government expenditure, gross fixed capital formation,

as well as for GDP. PPPs are also calculated for commodity groups such as food, clothing, housing, and expenditure on health and education.

A simple example of a PPP is the Big Mac index, which is compiled by *The Economist* magazine on a regular basis. According to *The Economist*'s web page on the Big Mac index accessed on 14 January 2020, the price of one Big Mac was HK$20.50 in Hong Kong, China; and 9.50 ringgit (RM) in Malaysia on the same date. If a Big Mac is the only item of interest, then the PPP between these two currencies is HK$1.00 = RM0.46.

The question is whether or not the Big Mac index is suitable or relevant as a PPP in general. In the example above, the price comparison is made on the basis of like with like, as a Big Mac is produced to the same specifications and quality in both Malaysia and Hong Kong, China. However, the Big Mac PPP cannot be used to convert household consumption expenditure as the Big Mac burger is not typically consumed in either of the two economies and does not represent the relevant consumption basket in either economy (in some developing economies, a Big Mac may even be considered a luxury item). Therefore, a PPP based on Big Mac prices is not useful for adjusting economy-level expenditures to account for the general price level differences and the subsequent conversion into a common currency unit.

Focusing on international comparisons of GDP and its components, if the PPP for Malaysian ringgit with the Hong Kong dollar as the reference currency is found to be 0.28—as was the case during the ICP's 2017 cycle (ADB 2020)—then RM28 is deemed to have the purchasing power equivalent of HK$100 when the basket of goods and services represents the whole of GDP. Thus, the PPP between Malaysian ringgit and the Hong Kong dollar can be used to convert GDP into real expenditure. As a result, the real expenditures in the two economies can be compared, and the differences in living standards can be assessed.

A note of caution is necessary in using and interpreting PPPs. In converting expenditure aggregates to eliminate price level differences, PPPs can be used. However, PPPs are not a direct measure of price levels between the two economies. In other words, a PPP of HK$1.00 = RM0.28 does not mean that prices in Malaysia are 28% of the observed prices in Hong Kong, China. It simply means that, in terms of currency units, you need RM0.28 to purchase the same set of items in Malaysia that can be purchased with HK$1.00 in Hong Kong, China. Are prices higher or cheaper in Malaysia relative to Hong Kong, China? This question is answered using the price level index.

Price Level Index

A measure of price levels, otherwise known as the price level index (PLI), for a given economy is defined as the ratio of PPP relative to the exchange rate of the currency, with respect to the numeraire or reference economy. If PPP at the GDP level between the Indian rupee (₹) and the Hong Kong dollar (HK$) is ₹3.43 = HK$1.00, and the market exchange rate is ₹8.36 = HK$1.00, then:

$$PLI \text{ for India} = \frac{\text{PPP for Indian rupee}}{\text{Exchange rate for Indian rupee}} \times 100$$

$$= \frac{3.43}{8.36} \times 100 = 41.03$$

This means that the price level in India at the GDP level is roughly 41% of that in Hong Kong, China. The concept behind the PLI is simple. If someone visiting India from Hong Kong, China exchanged HK$100 at the bank, they would receive ₹836 in exchange. However, what could be purchased for HK$100 in Hong Kong, China requires only ₹343 in India.

A few points are worth noting about PLIs.

- If the overall price level in India is 41% of that in Hong Kong, China, it may be that the prices in Hong Kong, China are relatively high or prices in

India are relatively low. The PLI by itself does not contain any information that can help identify the source of this low PLI for India. Therefore, PLIs are commonly expressed relative to the regional average, in this case Asia and the Pacific, which is given the value of 100. According to results from the ICP's 2017 cycle in the region, the PLI at the GDP level for Hong Kong, China was 156, while for India it was 64 (ADB 2020). This means that the price level in Hong Kong, China was 56% higher than the regional average in 2017, whereas the overall price level in India was 36% lower than the regional average.

- PLIs are influenced by both PPPs and exchange rates. Even if prices in both economies remain the same over time, and therefore the PPP remains at 3.43, a movement in the exchange rate can influence the PLI. For example, if the Indian rupee depreciates overnight and the new exchange rate is ₹10 = HK$1, then the PLI for India drops from 41 to 34, even though there were no changes in prices in India or in Hong Kong, China.

Key Measures

Gross Domestic Product

GDP is a measure of economic activity generated by the residents of an economy, and is defined as the market value of all final goods and services produced within the economy in a given period (e.g., in a year or a quarter). GDP is obtained by valuing goods and services at purchasers' prices that prevailed in the accounting period; and is described as GDP at current prices. The System of National Accounts 1993 was the framework used in the ICP's 2011 cycle, whereas its updated version—the System of National Accounts 2008—was the standard used in the ICP's 2017 cycle. This research study also used the System of National Accounts 2008.

There are three approaches to measuring GDP: production, income, and expenditure.

The production approach provides the most direct measure of GDP and is the sum of value-added (gross output *less* intermediate consumption of all the resident producer units in an economy *plus* any taxes less subsidies not already included in the value of the output). The production approach is the most common method of compiling GDP in many developing economies of Asia and the Pacific. However, it is difficult to make intereconomy comparisons of GDP using this approach in the ICP due to constraints in obtaining price data for both the outputs and intermediate inputs.

The income measure of GDP is the sum of compensation of employees, gross operating surplus (and mixed income of unincorporated enterprises), and taxes less subsidies on both production and imports. The income measure is also not used in international comparisons since prices for gross operating surplus are not available.

As it is relatively easier to collect price data for various expenditure components of GDP, the ICP uses the GDP measure from the expenditure side as the basis for international comparisons. The expenditure measure of GDP is the sum of expenditures on: (i) final consumption by households and government; (ii) gross capital formation; and (iii) balance of exports and imports. Government expenditure is divided into two components: expenditure by the government on behalf of households, such as on health and education; and collective consumption expenditure by the government, such as on defense, law and order, and other general activities of the government. The expenditure side of GDP can be written as:

individual consumption expenditure by households;

plus   individual consumption expenditure by nonprofit institutions serving households;

plus   government final consumption expenditure, which is composed of individual consumption expenditure by government and collective consumption expenditure by government;

plus   gross capital formation, which is composed of gross fixed capital formation and changes in inventories and acquisitions less disposals of valuables;

plus   balance of exports and imports (net exports).

Nominal Expenditures

Nominal expenditures are expenditures in different economies, expressed in their local currency units and converted into a common currency unit across all economies by using market exchange rates. As nominal expenditures do not reflect price level differences across economies, they cannot provide any comparable indication of living standards across economies.

Real Expenditures or Volumes

Real expenditures in different economies are obtained by converting expenditures in local currency units into a common currency unit while also adjusting for price level differences across economies. In other words, real expenditures are obtained by dividing the expenditures expressed in local currency units by their corresponding PPPs. It is important to note that PPPs specific to the expenditure component must be used in converting the corresponding expenditure in local currency units. When the price level differences between two economies have been accounted for through the use of PPPs, the resulting expenditure components are referred to as real expenditures that reflect the volumes of goods and services purchased in economies for international comparisons.

Expenditures Per Capita

The aggregate measure of real GDP is useful in measuring the size of an economy and its share in the regional or global economy. However, for purposes of comparing standards of living, it is appropriate to adjust real GDP to the size of the population. Real GDP per capita therefore provides a measure of standard of living. Similarly, other components of GDP, such as individual consumption expenditure by households, government final consumption expenditure, gross fixed capital formation, etc., when adjusted for population, provide measures that compare real expenditures per capita across economies for these measures.

Uses and Applications of Purchasing Power Parities

Since their emergence in the early 1970s, PPPs are now being used by a multitude of organizations and researchers in diverse areas.

The most common use of PPPs is to compile estimates of real GDP and real GDP per capita for comparison across economies. However, while per capita levels of real GDP and its various components are useful for many types of analyses, more robust estimates of real expenditure per capita are necessary to study the relative levels of, and disparities in, standards of living. Generally, such analyses focus on actual individual consumption by households rather than on GDP to compare standards of living and material well-being across economies.

As well as being important as an intermediate step in calculating the real values or volumes of GDP and its major components, PPPs are essential in calculating PLIs that enable comparisons of relative price levels across economies. While the PLI for GDP provides a measure of the overall price level in an economy, more specific PLIs provide valuable information on price levels for household consumption, gross fixed capital formation, and government final consumption expenditure, as well as for more disaggregated groupings such as food, clothing, and various types of services, including health and education. These PLIs provide valuable inputs for policymaking.

GDP figures converted using PPPs are used by the International Monetary Fund to help allocate quota subscriptions for member states, while the European Union uses PPP-converted GDP to allocate structural funds to its member states.

PPPs and PPP-converted aggregates have played a major role in the compilation of development indicators of global significance. The International Monetary Fund publishes, in its *World Economic Outlook*, estimates of annual global growth and inflation using weights that are based on PPP-converted GDP in different economies. ICP estimates of PPPs are also used in the construction of the Human Development Index, compiled and published annually through the *Human Development Report* of the United Nations Development Programme.

The World Bank, meanwhile, has used PPPs for household consumption as the basis for determining an international poverty line as an indicator of extreme poverty. Based on PPPs from the ICP's 1985 cycle, the international poverty line of $1 per day was calibrated for comparing extreme poverty across economies. This extreme poverty line was subsequently revised to $1.08 after the ICP's 1993 cycle, to $1.25 after the ICP's 2005 cycle, and to $1.90 after the release of PPP estimates from the ICP's 2011 cycle. The international extreme poverty line also formed the basis for the first Millennium Development Goal, proclaimed in 2000, to halve extreme poverty by 2015—a goal generally acknowledged to have been adequately met. PPPs have also featured prominently in measuring several targets of the Sustainable Development Goals set by the United Nations General Assembly in 2015, with $1.90 per day being the international poverty line set to measure Sustainable Development Goal 1, which is to eradicate extreme poverty for all people everywhere by 2030.

Other major areas where PPPs and PPP-converted real expenditures are used are to: (i) analyze convergence of prices and real incomes across economies;

(ii) measure and assess productivity performance at the sectoral and economy levels; (iii) measure levels and trends in inequality at the global level, and within and between regions; and (iv) calculate cost-of-living adjustments for employees working at overseas locations.

Caution in the Use of Purchasing Power Parities

PPPs are a powerful tool useful for a range of economic analyses. However, it is important to note that PPPs are not designed to indicate what the exchange rate of a currency should be. When the PPP theory was first developed, it was argued that PPPs would be close to "equilibrium exchange rates". It should be noted, though, that PPPs generated from ICP cycles cover both tradable and nontradable products, such as construction, personal services, and government services. Further, exchange rates are determined by the demand for a particular currency, and financing of foreign trade is only one component of this demand.

PPPs are statistics that are subject to a variety of errors, including sampling and nonsampling errors. National accounts statistics, which are used as weights in the calculation of PPPs, can also contain similar errors. The reliability of PPPs and estimated real expenditures (or volume measures) depends on the level of economic detail being assessed. At higher aggregate levels, such as GDP and household consumption, PPPs are likely to be more reliable, but they are potentially less reliable at more disaggregated levels, such as "food" or "bread and cereals". Some components of GDP are more challenging to compare than others. For example, nonmarket services—such as the provision of health, education, and other government services—remain difficult to compare across economies, despite concerted research efforts to address long-standing issues.

Finally, while PPPs are of considerable use in studying and analyzing the size and structure of the global economy, it is important to recognize that such measures for different baskets of goods and services are likely to differ significantly. It is vital to identify the correct economic aggregate and apply its corresponding PPP to study a given problem. Users must also be cautious about applying PPPs published at different points in time. Such estimates cannot be used directly in making statements about price levels in a given economy over time, because prices of the comparable commodities, relative to those in the reference economy, may have significantly changed over time.

3. Framework and Methodology for Compiling Purchasing Power Parities

The general framework and methodology followed in the implementation of the International Comparison Program (ICP) is endorsed by the Technical Advisory Group of the ICP. The Technical Advisory Group comprises experts in the areas of index numbers, purchasing power parities (PPPs), price statistics, and national accounts statistics. This group is entrusted with ensuring methodological soundness and overall quality in compiling the PPP estimates and steering the ICP research agenda.

This report considers the general framework and methods used in the construction of PPPs for ICP benchmark years, and presents a review of options for estimating PPPs in the years between benchmark cycles.

Fundamental Decomposition of National Accounts Aggregates

The main objective of the ICP is to provide internationally comparable data on gross domestic product (GDP) and its components, as compiled by national statistics offices and following international standards on national accounts statistics—most recently the United Nations System of National Accounts 2008 (United Nations 2009). The starting point for the ICP is the observed GDP in each economy, expressed in the local currency unit. The ICP provides a decomposition of the GDP into quantity and price components, which can be written as:

$$\text{GDP in economy } j \text{ (in local currency unit)} = Q_j \times P_j$$

where Q_j represents the quantity component of GDP in economy j, which is usually referred to as a volume measure or the real GDP; and P_j represents the price component in economy j.

As the ICP makes comparisons across economies, the price component is referred to as the PPP for the currency of economy j (PPP_j), which provides the means of converting the GDP of economy j from its local currency unit to a common currency unit. Thus, we have:

$$\text{GDP in economy } j \text{ (in local currency unit)} = \text{Real } GDP_j \times PPP_j = Volume_j \times PPP_j$$

In summary, the ICP provides estimates of:

- PPPs of currencies of the participating economies,
- volume measures or real measures of GDP, and
- PPPs and volume measures for the components of GDP.

General Framework of the International Comparison Program

The ICP uses a hierarchical approach whereby PPPs are estimated at the lowest level of aggregation and then progressively aggregated to yield PPPs for higher-level components of GDP, ultimately leading to PPPs and volume measures at the overall GDP level. Figure 3.1 shows the bottom-up approach for the compilation of PPPs, which starts with data on prices of individual goods and services that are then grouped into basic headings to form higher-level aggregates—classes, groups, categories, main aggregates, and finally, GDP.

The two key steps of classifying GDP components are basic headings and the higher-level aggregates.

Figure 3.1: Hierarchical Structure for Main Components of Gross Domestic Product

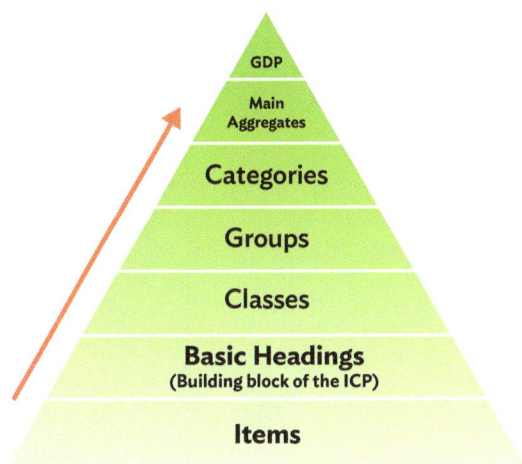

GDP = gross domestic product, ICP = International Comparison Program.
Source: D.S.P. Rao. 2013. The Framework of the International Comparison Program. In *Measuring the Real Size of the World Economy*, edited by World Bank. Washington, DC: World Bank.

Basic Headings

The basic heading is the building block for the compilation of PPPs and real aggregates. These basic headings have three important characteristics. First, a basic heading is a set of items that are expected to be homogeneous, covering similar well-defined goods or services. In practice, however, some basic headings may cover a broader range of items. Second, the relative prices of goods or services within a basic heading are expected to be similar across economies. Third, the basic heading is the lowest-level expenditure component of GDP at which expenditure data from the national accounts are required. These data provide weights for calculating PPPs above the basic-heading level.

Higher-Level Aggregates

Higher-level aggregates are composed of at least one basic heading. Table 3.1 shows the composition and aggregation of basic headings to form higher-level aggregates based on the ICP classification used in this research study.

The ICP identifies a total of 155 basic headings within the GDP composite. As mentioned, the basic heading is the first level of aggregation for which PPPs are compiled, before being aggregated into higher levels of PPPs. These higher levels comprise 126 classes, 63 groups, 28 categories, 6 main aggregates, and, finally, the composite level GDP. Higher-level PPPs are compiled by a weighted aggregation of the PPPs at their basic-heading levels, weights being the corresponding expenditures in the GDP.

The six main aggregates under GDP are:

- Individual consumption expenditure by households (ICEH),
- Individual consumption expenditure by nonprofit institutions serving households (ICENPISH),
- Individual consumption expenditure by government (ICEG),
- Collective consumption expenditure by government (CCEG),
- Gross capital formation (GCF), and
- Balance of exports and imports (or net exports).

Table 3.1 shows that the main aggregate ICEH comprises 110 of the 155 basic headings. It can also be seen that ICEH is made up of 13 categories (food and nonalcoholic beverages; alcoholic beverages, narcotics, and tobacco; clothing and footwear; and so on). Similarly, the main aggregate GCF comprises three categories; namely, gross fixed capital formation, changes in inventories, and acquisitions less disposals of valuables.

In addition to these standard national accounts aggregates, the ICP focuses on two additional aggregates that can be formed out of the six main aggregates listed. The first additional aggregate is actual individual consumption by households (AICH), which includes ICEH, ICENPISH, and ICEG. The second special aggregate is domestic absorption, which includes all the major aggregates except net exports.

Table 3.1: Composition of Main Aggregates of Gross Domestic Product Used in the Study

	Main Aggregates or Categories	Category	Group	Class	Basic Heading
	Gross Domestic Product	28	63	126	155
1100000	Individual Consumption Expenditure by Households	13	44	91	110
1101000	Food and nonalcoholic beverages		2	11	29
1102000	Alcoholic beverages, tobacco, and narcotics		3	5	5
1103000	Clothing and footwear		2	5	5
1104000	Housing, water, electricity, gas, and other fuels		5	8	8
1105000	Furnishings, household equipment, and routine household maintenance		6	12	13
1106000	Health		3	7	7
1107000	Transport		3	13	13
1108000	Communication		3	3	3
1109000	Recreation and culture		6	13	13
1110000	Education		1	1	1
1111000	Restaurants and hotels		2	2	2
1112000	Miscellaneous goods and services		7	10	10
1113000	Net purchases abroad		1	1	1
1200000	Individual Consumption Expenditure by NPISHs	5	5	5	5
1201000	Housing		1	1	1
1202000	Health		1	1	1
1203000	Recreation and culture		1	1	1
1204000	Education		1	1	1
1205000	Social protection and other services		1	1	1
1300000	Individual Consumption Expenditure by Government	5	7	16	21
1301000	Housing		1	1	1
1302000	Health		2	7	12
1303000	Recreation and culture		1	1	1
1304000	Education		2	6	6
1305000	Social protection		1	1	1
1400000	Collective Consumption Expenditure by Government	1	1	5	5
1500000	Gross Capital Formation	3	5	8	12
1501000	Gross fixed capital formation		3	6	10
1502000	Changes in inventories		1	1	1
1503000	Acquisitions less disposals of valuables		1	1	1
1600000	Balance of Exports and Imports	1	1	1	2

NPISHs = nonprofit institutions serving households.

Note: The classification used is the same as the one used for the 2017 ICP and 2011 ICP revised results.

Source: Asian Development Bank based on World Bank. 2016. *International Comparison Program: Classification of Final Expenditure on GDP.* Washington, DC. http://pubdocs. worldbank.org/en/708531575560035925/pdf/ICP-Classification-description-2019-1205.pdf.

AICH is recommended as an appropriate measure of consumption by households when comparisons of standards of living are made across economies. For example, an economy may have high GDP per capita; but, if a large portion of GDP is formed by gross fixed capital formation, then household consumption levels would be low. Further, AICH accounts for contributions to household consumption by the government and nonprofit institutions serving households, through their expenditure on housing, health, recreation and culture, education, and social protection.

Domestic absorption provides a measure that covers consumption, investment, and government expenditure within a given economy. Domestic absorption is a meaningful aggregate to compare across economies because it makes an adjustment for economies with high levels of net exports, which is usually the case with resource-rich economies.

There have been some revisions to the classification of basic headings since the ICP's 2011 cycle, and this revised classification was used in the 2017 cycle. It may be noted that, for comparability, the ICP results for 2011 were also revised following the new ICP classification. The new classification, as used in the ICP's 2017 cycle, was also employed in this research study (Appendix 3).

Compiling Purchasing Power Parities: Data Collection and Validation

The process of compiling PPPs is very similar to that used in the regular compilation of the consumer price index (CPI). The CPI makes use of price data collected on goods and services that are purchased by consumers at different points in time. This price information is then aggregated to calculate the CPI for major expenditure components within the consumer basket—such components include food, clothing, housing, health, education, transport, other commodities—and for the household consumption expenditure as a whole. The compilation of PPPs under the ICP is similar, but with two important distinctions. First, it covers much more than just household consumption: it also covers GCF, government consumption expenditure, and net exports—these are all components of GDP. Second, while CPI is an index for temporal comparison

of prices in an economy, PPPs are indexes for spatial comparison of prices across economies.

There are two major data requirements for the compilation of PPPs and real GDP. The first concerns the collection of comparable price data for a basket of comparable goods and services, while the second is GDP expenditure data from national accounts statistics sourced from each participating economy. The prices and national accounts data should be comparable, consistent, and based on the standard concepts, classifications, and practices underlying the System of National Accounts 2008. These two major data requirements are discussed below.

Collection of Relevant and Consistent Price Data

The first major step in any ICP cycle is the collection of annual average prices for a basket of specified products within participating economies. There are several elements involved in the collection of price data for each ICP cycle, including:

- preparation of standardized product lists for price collection,
- design of an appropriate survey framework and collection of prices,
- validation and editing of price data, and
- calculation of annual average prices for the products.

Product Lists for Collecting Price Data

The first step in ICP work is the preparation of a list of products (goods and services) whose prices are to be collected in all participating economies across a particular region. The product lists are prepared separately for household consumption; government consumption; and components of gross fixed capital formation, including construction, and machinery and equipment. No price data are collected for exports and imports as exchange rates are used as PPP measures for this component of GDP.

To ensure consistency and comparability across all ICP regions, determination of product lists at the regional level needs to be consistent with the decisions made at the ICP Global Office. However, the ICP's regional implementing agencies have a major role to play as the program is regionalized and price comparisons need to be meaningful across participating economies in the region. Thus, both global and regional considerations influence the product lists for price surveys.

The following are the major considerations that underpin product list preparations for ICP price surveys across Asia and the Pacific:

Comparability. Since PPPs represent measures of relative prices in different economies, it is necessary to ensure that the products priced are themselves comparable, i.e., they have very similar characteristics that determine price. Products selected should therefore be sufficiently well specified, so that prices collected in different economies for these products are comparable. However, strict adherence to comparability criteria can often result in narrowly specified products.

Representativity and importance. The products priced in different economies should be representative of the consumption and investment patterns in each respective economy. If products are narrowly specified, the products become comparable but may not always be representative or relevant. A careful balance between these two competing considerations, comparability and representativity, needs to be achieved in the preparation of product lists. Achieving this balance is facilitated through regional workshops, organized by the Asian Development Bank (ADB) as the regional implementing agency, and drawing on the expertise of price statisticians from participating economies.

Structured product descriptions. For all goods and services included in the product lists for price surveys, a detailed specification of products—a structured product description—is created. These descriptions capture as many price-determining characteristics as possible to ensure collection of prices of comparable products.

The selection of items and the survey framework for this research study used a "reduced information approach," which differs from the standard practice for ICP benchmark cycles. A more detailed description of the study's methodology is provided in Chapter 4.

Annual Economy-Wide Average Prices

The prices used in PPP calculations should be based on annual economy-wide average prices. Since PPPs are to be used in converting annual aggregates for GDP and its components for a given reference year (the 2016 calendar year in the case of this research study), the prices of listed products must represent the entire reference year. Similarly, as GDP is calculated for a whole economy, prices must reflect the average prices paid for the products in different geographic areas of the economy.

Price surveys must therefore be designed to capture economy-wide annual average prices, covering both rural and urban areas. If the products are seasonal, surveys must be conducted in different seasons, then be appropriately weighted to yield meaningful annual averages. As it is usually difficult to calculate weighted averages of price quotations collected, where feasible, the price surveys must use self-weighted designs so that simple averages of price quotations provide reliable estimates of economy-wide average prices. If the self-weighting design reflects the volumes of sales in different locations, a simple arithmetic average is appropriate.

The approach used to arrive at annual economy-wide average prices for this research study is discussed in Chapter 4.

Editing and Validation of Price Data

The quality of price and GDP data is crucial to the calculation of reliable PPPs. Considerable resources are allocated to review and validate the data supplied by all participating economies, ensuring consistency of prices within economies as well as comparability of prices across economies. Accordingly, validation of data is undertaken at two different levels (ADB 2020).

- At the economy level, individual price quotations are checked for the presence of outliers, to ensure pricing of comparable products across different outlets and geographic areas (intraeconomy validation). Economy-wide average prices, along with the number of quotations, standard deviations, coefficient of variations, and minimum and maximum prices, form the basis of data validation at this level.
- At the regional level, average prices submitted by participating economies are validated using a range of cross-economy methods using Dikhanov tables (intereconomy validation).

Similar methods of price validation were followed in this research study using software applications developed by ADB and the World Bank.

Aggregation of Price Data and Expenditure Data from National Accounts

The second requirement as input to compiling PPPs is GDP expenditure data broken down into the 155 basic headings and following standard classification by all participating economies. PPPs from the ICP are used to convert national accounts aggregates in different economies into a common currency unit. It is therefore important that the price data collected for different products belonging to different national accounts aggregates and components are consistent with the international standard practices of national accounts statistics. This also implies that the prices collected under the ICP should correspond to the pricing concepts used in the compilation of value aggregates by national accountants. If prices collected and pricing concepts do not correspond, the resulting volume measures are likely to be incorrect and biased.

In their national accounts publications, most economies usually classify final expenditures on GDP into far fewer components than the 155 basic headings required under the ICP. For these economies, providing expenditure weights or expenditures at the detailed level is a major undertaking. In many cases, expenditures at higher levels of aggregation need to be split. A variety of sources—including expenditure weights taken from CPIs, household expenditure surveys, government expenditure accounts, and capital expenditure surveys—are used. In some cases, economies use weights that had been calculated for earlier cycles of the ICP.

For this research study, the data requirements for GDP expenditure according to the 155 basic headings were the same as those of a regular ICP benchmark cycle and followed the 2017 ICP classification.

Validation of GDP Expenditure Data

GDP expenditure data for different categories and components are compared across participating economies. At the initial stage, the regional implementing agency identifies gaps and inconsistencies in the data at the economy level. Such discrepancies include not providing disaggregation by basic headings, not satisfying the reverse mathematical operations, and subcomponents not adding up to totals.

The processes described above are designed to ensure that the prices and national accounts data—the basic input data for the calculation of PPPs—are of high quality, thereby ensuring the high quality of compiled PPPs and corresponding real expenditures.

Compiling Purchasing Power Parities: Methods Used by the International Comparison Program

The main outputs of any ICP cycle are the PPPs of currencies of economies in the region and the corresponding estimates of real GDP and its components. The calculation of PPPs is an intermediate step toward obtaining internationally comparable national income aggregates.

Calculations of PPPs for intereconomy price comparisons are undertaken in the following two steps:

- (Unweighted) PPPs at the basic-heading level are calculated for every basic heading, using price data for the individual items in the basic heading (in the absence of expenditure weights associated with individual items). Other methods are used to estimate PPPs for the basic headings under which no prices are available for individual items.
- Higher-level PPP aggregations are calculated, where basic-heading level PPPs are aggregated using expenditure shares from national accounts as weights.

Methods of aggregating price data differ for the basic headings and higher-level aggregations.

Calculation of Purchasing Power Parities at the Basic-Heading Level

At the recommendation of the ICP's Technical Advisory Group in 2011, the country-product-dummy (CPD) method is used in calculating PPPs at the basic-heading level. The CPD method is a generalized multilateral method that uses a regression technique to obtain transitive PPPs for each basic heading. The regression model reflects the law of "one price," which means that the observed price of a commodity in a given economy is essentially the product of an international average price of the commodity and the general price level in the economy. Data for a given basic heading consist of the observed prices of all available products within the basic heading for all participating economies in the region.

Consider a basic heading which has N items. Let p_{ij} be the observed or reported price of commodity i in jth economy $\{i = 1,2,...,N; j = 1,2,...,M\}$. Conceptually, every p_{ij} can be decomposed into a commodity-specific factor, η_i; an economy-specific factor, π_j; and

a factor of ε_{ij} to account for the deviation of $\eta_i \times \pi_j$ from the actual price p_{ij}:

$$p_{ij} = \eta_i \times \pi_j \times \varepsilon_{ij}$$

Taking natural logarithms, the model can be expressed in the form of a regression model with economy and commodity fixed effects using dummy variables. The model then takes the form:

$$\ln p_{ij} = \ln \eta_i + \ln \pi_j + \ln \varepsilon_{ij}$$
$$= \sum_{n=1}^{N} \eta_n D_n^* + \sum_{m=1}^{M} \pi_m D_m + u_{ij}$$

where p_{ij} is the annual average price of ith product reported by economy j. D_n^* and D_m are product and economy dummy variables, respectively. The last term, u_{ij} is a random disturbance term.

The CPD method estimates this regression model using the simple "least squares" method, after imposing a restriction on one parameter, as the model exhibits perfect multicollinearity. Since Hong Kong, China is chosen as the reference economy in Asia and the Pacific, the CPD model is estimated imposing the restriction that the economy coefficient for Hong Kong, China is set to zero, i.e., $\pi_{HKG} = 0$. Once the parameters of the model are estimated, PPPs for the remaining economies, with Hong Kong, China as the base economy, are estimated by:

$$PPP_j = exp(\hat{\pi}_j) \text{ for } j = 1,2,...,M$$

The CPD method has several major advantages. It can be applied in the most practical scenario, where not all commodities are priced in all economies, and it makes use of all price data available. The CPD model also makes it possible to attach weights to price observations. For example, if a particular commodity is deemed to be representative or important, it is possible to attach a higher weight for such commodities. In fact, the ICP's Technical Advisory Group recommended that all products identified as important be given a weight of 3, compared to a weight of 1 for unimportant products or those that are not representative.

However, identifying the importance of products is not straightforward and it is subject to interpretation by the implementing agencies from the participating economies. Accordingly, as in the ICP's 2005, 2011, and 2017 cycles, this research study opted not to use any information on importance of products priced.

Reference Purchasing Power Parities for Selected Basic Headings

For several basic headings, it is not possible to obtain prices that match directly with the aggregates. "Acquisitions less disposals of valuables" and "changes in inventories" are examples of such basic headings. Similarly, no price data are used for net exports. Indirect PPPs are used for these kinds of basic headings and these measures are called "reference PPPs". Generally, reference PPPs are taken from another related basic heading or a combination of related basic headings, or they are alternatively referenced to the PPP of a suitably identified aggregate. In the case of net exports, exchange rates are used as reference PPPs. The reference PPPs for changes in inventories are the PPPs for basic headings classified as containing predominantly goods (both consumer and investment). Appendix 2 provides a list of the reference PPPs used in this research study.

Calculation of Purchasing Power Parities for Higher-Level Aggregates

After calculating PPPs for the 155 basic headings, the regional implementing agency compiles a complete table of PPPs for all basic headings for all participating economies (20 economies in the case of this research study), along with national accounts expenditure data corresponding to each basic heading for all participating economies. The basic heading PPPs are treated like price data associated with the composite group of items that the basic heading represents. To implement the index number formulas below, the following data structure is available:

$$\{p_{ij}, e_{ij}: i = 1,2,\dots,155 \text{ and } j = 1,2,\dots,20\}$$

where p_{ij} and e_{ij} are, respectively, price (PPP) and expenditure (in local currency units) for ith basic heading in jth economy.

To calculate PPPs at higher levels of aggregation, it is necessary first to identify the component of interest, then consider all the basic headings that make up this component. If the component "food and nonalcoholic beverages" is of interest, then it is necessary to include all 29 basic headings that this aggregate comprises. Similarly, if GDP is of interest, then all 155 basic headings must be included. The formulas given below are for GDP as a whole, but the same formula applied to different sets of basic headings can be used for other analytical components.

Since the ICP's 2005 cycle, the program's Technical Advisory Group has recommended using the Gini-Éltető-Köves-Szulc (GEKS) method as the index number method to calculate PPPs for aggregates at levels above the basic heading. The GEKS method builds on the well-known Fisher binary index number formula, chosen because it satisfies a number of axiomatic and economic theoretic properties, including the country reversal test, factor reversal test, and commensurability test. The Fisher index is also known to be superlative from an economic theoretic viewpoint (Diewert 2013).

$$\text{Fisher index} = F_{jk} = \left[L_{jk} \times P_{jk}\right]^{1/2}$$

$$= \left[\left(\sum_{i=1}^{155} \frac{p_{ik}}{p_{ij}} \times e_{ij}\right) \times \frac{1}{\left(\sum_{i=1}^{155} \frac{p_{ij}}{p_{ik}} \times e_{ik}\right)}\right]^{1/2}$$

where $e_{ij} = \frac{p_{ij} \times q_{ij}}{\sum_{i=1}^{155} p_{ij} \times q_{ij}}$ is share of ith basic heading in the GDP of the jth economy.

Under the GEKS method, PPPs are calculated in two stages. In the first stage, the Fisher binary index, denoted by F_{jk}, is calculated for each pair of economies, j and k, as the geometric mean of the Laspeyres and Paasche price indexes denoted, respectively, L_{jk} and P_{jk}.

This Fisher index is not transitive and therefore cannot be used for international comparisons. The GEKS formula for calculating the PPP for economy k with economy j as the base, considering 20 economies participating in this research study, is:

$$PPP_{jk} = \prod_{l=1}^{20}\left[F_{jl} \times F_{lk}\right]^{\frac{1}{20}} \text{ for } j,k = 1,2,\dots,20$$

The GEKS index provides PPPs that are transitive and base invariant and at the same time, by construction, close to the Fisher binary index. Therefore, the GEKS index also possesses the property of characteristicity.

The GEKS procedure has been used in all ICP cycles since 2005 and was also adopted for this research study.

A Caution on Non-Additivity of Real Expenditures

The national accounts aggregates expressed in respective local currency units are additive in the sense that lower-level components add up to higher-level aggregates. When these aggregates are converted using exchange rates, the resulting nominal aggregates are also additive. Thus, the nominal values of the six main aggregates sum to nominal GDP. This is because the same exchange rate is used for converting all the aggregates. In the case of real expenditures, different PPPs are used to convert different components, thus resulting in non-additivity of real expenditures of main categories to the real GDP. For example, the PPP used to convert ICEH in local currency units into real ICEH is different from the PPP used to convert ICEG or GDP. This non-additivity of real aggregates has to be recognized when interpreting results.

Compilation of Purchasing Power Parities between Benchmark Cycles: Options

The ICP benchmarks provide snapshots of the regional economy for a given year, with estimates of the PPPs of currencies, price levels, and real expenditures, as well as estimates of GDP and its components. Since 1970, the uses and applications of results from the ICP have assumed significance among international organizations, researchers, and policymakers, leading to an increasing demand for internationally comparable economic aggregates on an annual basis. Despite this demand, the ICP benchmark cycles have remained infrequent, available roughly 5 to 6 years apart, mainly due to the complexity and resource-intensive nature of conducting each cycle. The World Bank's *World Development Indicators* and the Penn World Tables are currently the main sources of data on PPPs and real expenditures on annual basis.

The need to increase the frequency of ICP cycles has been recognized by the United Nations Statistical Commission, which recommended in its 47th session that ICP cycles be conducted every 3 years. The Statistical Office of the European Communities (Eurostat) conducts international comparisons on an annual basis, using the rolling price survey approach; while the Organisation for Economic Co-operation and Development conducts comparisons and publishes results every 3 years.

The need to fill the gaps in information between ICP cycles has long been recognized by ADB. Shortly after the results of the ICP's 2005 cycle were published, the bank started working on initiatives to address the issue of extrapolation, improve operational aspects of ICP cycles, and reduce the data collection burden and related costs to the implementing agencies of the participating economies. ADB then conducted a research project to explore the possibility of using a reduced information approach to construct PPPs for years between benchmark cycles, using the interim year of 2009 as an example. This research study based on 2016 data is a continuation of the research efforts of the 2009 study, and is again designed to produce a snapshot of the Asia and Pacific region for a year between ICP benchmarks.

The challenge in its most general form is how to provide more frequent and reliable estimates of real expenditures and price levels for participating economies of the region, by doing so on an annual basis or at least more frequently than the current 6-year period between ICP cycles.[1] Meeting this challenge may be possible through various options and alternative approaches.

Option 1: Conducting a Full International Comparison Program Annually

Compiling annual PPPs and real aggregates would be a fairly simple task if there were no constraints on resources available for conducting the ICP's full-scale exercise. Under this scenario, the participating economies, the regional implementing agencies, and the ICP Global Office would simply replicate the tasks involved in the benchmark comparisons, say the 2011 or 2017 cycle, leading to a new set of PPPs for each new benchmark year. In terms of data requirements, the participating economies would provide: (i) prices from the regional product lists; (ii) prices for items in the global core list; (iii) expenditure weights for the 155 basic headings drawn from national accounts; and (iv) other auxiliary data such as population. These data are then aggregated at various levels following standard ICP methods, ultimately leading to price and real expenditure comparisons for GDP and other aggregates at the regional and global levels.

While this option is highly resource intensive, it has some merits. The regional and economy-level implementing agencies would be able to plan ahead

and integrate ICP-related tasks with domestic CPI price collection, benefiting from synergies between the two processes. Currently, the World Bank is developing a set of operational guidelines to help the participating economies achieve a higher level of integration of CPI and ICP activities. However, to implement these guidelines in a sustainable manner, dedicated financial and human resources will have to be allocated to manage the added burden of data collection and data processing at all levels.

Option 2: Use of a Rolling Benchmark Approach

The use of a "rolling benchmark" approach to collecting ICP prices is designed to spread the burden of price collection over a 3-year period. It involves pricing approximately one-sixth of the household products in each of the 6 half-years over the period. The annual average prices of ICP items are then estimated by using changes in the corresponding CPI product prices, to adjust them to the price level of the benchmark year. This procedure is being used successfully by the Organisation for Economic Co-operation and Development and Eurostat in their joint PPP program. The obvious advantage of this option is that the workload for ICP price collection is spread more evenly over time, rather than concentrated in a single year. In addition, estimates of PPPs and real expenditures for the years between benchmark years become more accurate. This option was proposed by the Friends of the Chair Group (ECOSOC 2016a), which evaluated the ICP's 2011 cycle, and was also agreed by the United Nations Statistical Commission in its 47th session in 2016 (ECOSOC 2016b). The ICP Global Office is developing a position paper on the use of a "rolling price survey approach" for consideration by the regional implementing agencies. The approach being canvassed is to facilitate an increase in the frequency of ICP cycles to 3 years by replacing the benchmark approach and to provide more frequent estimates of PPPs. The experience of Eurostat

---

[1]   Following the recommendations of the United Nations Statistical Commission in 2016, ICP is now gearing toward conducting its cycles on a global scale every 3 years, although the ICP's 2020 cycle was postponed to 2021 due to the impacts of the COVID-19 pandemic.

demonstrates that this approach can be successfully used, although the regional implementing agencies will need to carefully study the data requirements, technical considerations, resources needed, and capacity of participating economies to implement this approach in their respective regions.

Option 3: Extrapolation at Aggregate Level

A standard approach of compiling PPPs for years other than the ICP cycles or benchmarks is simply to extrapolate the estimates from a given cycle to the desired year, using price changes in each economy relative to the reference economy. This is the approach used in the *World Development Indicators* and the Penn World Tables.

The System of National Accounts 2008 formally describes the method commonly used to extrapolate PPPs from a benchmark year as follows:

The method commonly used to extrapolate PPPs from their benchmark year to another year is to use the ratio of the national accounts deflators from each country compared with a numeraire country (generally the United States of America) to move each country's PPPs forward from the benchmark. The PPPs derived are then applied to the relevant national accounts component to obtain volumes expressed in a common currency for the year in question.

Theoretically, the best means of extrapolating PPPs from a benchmark year would be to use time series of prices at the individual product level from each country in the CPI to extrapolate the prices of the individual products included in the ICP benchmark. In practice, it is not possible to use this type of procedure in extrapolating PPP benchmarks because the detailed price data needed are not available in all the countries. Therefore, an approach based on extrapolating at a macro level (for GDP or for a handful of GDP components) is generally adopted. Leaving aside the data problems involved in collecting consistent data

from all the countries involved, a major conceptual question arises with this process because it can be demonstrated mathematically that it is impossible to maintain consistency across both time and space. In other words, extrapolating PPPs using time series of prices at a broad level such as GDP will not result in a match with the benchmark PPP-based estimates even if all the data are perfectly consistent (United Nations 2009, 322).

The extrapolation method has the advantage of being simple to implement, and the data required are readily available for any economy that has a set of annual national accounts. In many cases, extrapolated PPPs obtained using the conventional method are good approximations of those obtained from a benchmark, so they fit in well between two benchmark cycles. However, this method's disadvantage is that the extrapolated PPPs may be inaccurate in some cases, because assumptions behind the process are restrictive and may not be met in practice.

To extrapolate PPPs at the GDP level, GDP deflators are used. Let PPP of economy j, at the GDP level, at time point t be denoted by PPP_j^t. Further, let the GDP deflators, representing price changes at the GDP level from period t to $t+1$ in economy j and the reference economy R be, respectively, denoted by $Def_j^{t,t+1}$ and $Def_R^{t,t+1}$. Then, the extrapolated PPP is simply given by:

$$PPP_j^{t+1} = PPP_j^t \times \frac{Def_j^{t,t+1}}{Def_R^{t,t+1}}$$

This is a simple procedure that relies only on the data supplied by the economies on price deflators. This procedure produces PPPs that are transitive and base invariant. Once the PPPs are extrapolated, real expenditures can be calculated by converting expenditures in local currency units into the currency of the reference economy using extrapolated PPPs.

This procedure of extrapolating PPPs can be applied at any desired level of aggregation. Though commonly used to extrapolate PPPs at the GDP level, and for major components such as ICEH, government final consumption expenditure, and gross fixed capital formation, this procedure can be applied to PPPs for lower-level aggregates such as food, clothing, transportation, and machinery and equipment; or, even at the level of the basic heading. The main data requirement for this procedure is the availability of reliable and appropriate deflators at the level desired.

While this option is simple to use, it does raise some practical considerations. The most important issue is the possible inconsistency between two successive benchmarks and the extrapolated PPPs and real expenditures generated following this procedure using deflators. Suppose extrapolations are made by applying this procedure to GDP and other aggregates from 2011 in order to compile PPP estimates for 2012, 2013, and so on up to 2017. For 2017, PPPs and real expenditures are available from the ICP's 2017 cycle. The question then is: would the 2017 extrapolations of PPPs based on deflators match the PPPs compiled through the complete ICP process for the benchmark year 2017? In general, the answer is no. In fact, sometimes the differences can be significant. For example, at the conclusion of the ICP's 2011 cycle, it was found that the PPPs for the 2011 benchmark differed significantly and systematically from PPPs obtained by extrapolating PPPs from the 2005 cycle to 2011. In fact, for most low-income economies, the PPPs from the 2011 cycle were lower than the PPPs extrapolated from the 2005 benchmark. These discrepancies were the subject of studies by Deaton and Aten (2017) and Inklaar and Rao (2017).

McCarthy (2013) and Inklaar and Timmer (2013) offer more general explanations for the divergence between benchmark results and extrapolations. They suggest that the PPPs obtained by extrapolating from a benchmark using time series data will almost certainly differ from those calculated in a full ICP cycle. Both conceptual and practical challenges contribute to these differences. Dalgaard and Sørensen (2002) showed that it is conceptually not possible to match PPPs extrapolated using time series national accounts with PPPs from an ICP benchmark year. They concluded that "...it is not reasonable to say that PPP benchmarks and national price and volume data are 'inconsistent' when they fail to satisfy simultaneous transitivity across space and time" (Dalgaard and Sørensen 2002, 4). Ideally, to minimize any such differences, PPPs would be extrapolated from the benchmark year, say 2011, using detailed price data at the level of the 155 basic headings. However, economies do not have consistent time series price indexes at this very detailed level for years between the benchmarks, and therefore extrapolation is generally based only on the deflator for GDP. At best, it should be based on using deflators for a handful of major components of GDP, using the extrapolation formula.

The main assumptions underlying the process of simply extrapolating a benchmark PPP using the relationship between changes in different economies' GDP deflators are: that economies have similar economic structures as in the benchmark year; and that their structures change at the same rate over time. These are very restrictive assumptions.

In addition, the weights applied to the individual price indexes that are combined to produce GDP deflators in the national accounts time series will change over time and these changes will not be identical between the economies involved in the extrapolation process. Prices used in the GDP deflators will be different from those in the PPP benchmarks for GDP. In a time series, the main requirement is that prices collected should be for similar products to be priced over time. Quality adjustments are applied to the time series price indexes to take into account changes in product specifications over time. On the other hand, the main requirement in spatial price indexes is for the products priced to be representative within each economy and comparable between economies. This means that the basket of products priced for the ICP may be different from those in each economy's national accounts time series.

Another potential issue arises if an economy's terms of trade change markedly over time, because the extrapolation method assumes that changes in prices due to changes in the terms of trade are price effects, whereas they are treated as volume effects in a benchmark PPP. The study of Varjonen (2002) provides a good overview of some inconsistencies between ICP benchmarks and extrapolated GDP figures. In his paper, Varjonen reports inconsistencies arising between benchmark and extrapolated PPPs ranging from –13.6% for Turkey to 11.7% for Greece during 1990–1999. The paper by Dalgaard and Sørensen (2002) also highlights some large discrepancies between the benchmark and extrapolated series for some economies, but notes that revisions made in national accounts data after the benchmark PPPs were calculated are at least partly responsible for the magnitude of discrepancy.

Despite limitations in the current extrapolation methodology, some useful results can still be obtained using this option, provided the years extrapolated are not too far from the benchmark year. It is in this context that this ADB research study—along with the 2009 update project—attempts to provide a more firmly based set of PPPs than could be obtained using the simple and broad-level extrapolation procedure, by aiming to address or avoid the limitations of the conventional extrapolation methodology.

Option 4: Extrapolation at Disaggregated Level and Aggregation

Option 3 shows that extrapolated PPPs are likely to differ from the benchmark PPPs due to a variety of factors, including expenditure weights, formulas used for the calculation of PPPs, the products priced in different benchmark years, and the products included in the compilation of domestic deflators.

Option 4 attempts to answer the question about the desired level at which extrapolations should be made. More specifically, should statistics practitioners be extrapolating PPPs directly at the GDP level, at the level of household consumption, at the level of commodity groups such as "food" and "clothing," or at the level of the basic headings (the lowest level at which PPPs are calculated before being aggregated to higher levels)?

The option under discussion is anchored on the work of Deaton (2012) and draws on the analysis of Inklaar and Rao (2019). The analysis uses the simplest of cases involving only two economies and two time periods, instead of the complex multilateral price comparisons for the ICP involving a very large number of economies. Despite this simplicity of analysis, the method has useful practical implications.

Consider the simple case of two economies where PPP is calculated using the Törnqvist index number formula.[2] Since there are only two economies, it is sufficient to use a binary index such as the Törnqvist index. Now, suppose that the same set of commodities enter into PPP and economy-wide price index calculations. To make the illustration simple, expenditure shares of commodities are assumed to differ across economies but remain the same over time periods t and $t+1$. Let p_{ij}^s represent the price of the ith commodity ($i = 1,2,...,N$) in jth economy ($j = 1,2$) in period s ($s = t, t+1$). Let e_{ij} represent expenditure shares associated with commodity i in economy j. We also let PPP_2^s represent the PPP of the currency of economy 2 with economy 1 as the reference economy in period s. Let P_j represent the price index in economy j over time from t to $t+1$. Then, the natural logarithmic form of the three Törnqvist indexes are given by:

$$\ln PPP_2^s = \frac{1}{2}\sum_{i=1}^{N}(e_{i1} + e_{i2})(\ln p_{i2}^s - \ln p_{i1}^s) \text{ for } s = t, t+1$$

---

2   This formula is selected in preference to the Fisher index, due to the analytical simplicity it offers. Further, Fisher and Törnqvist indices produce numerically close PPPs.

$$\ln P_2 = \sum_{i=1}^{N} e_{i2}(\ln p_{i2}^{t+1} - \ln p_{i2}^{t})$$

$$\ln P_1 = \sum_{i=1}^{N} e_{i1}(\ln p_{i1}^{t+1} - \ln p_{i1}^{t})$$

It is easy to see that PPP_2^s is a Törnqvist index that compares price levels across economies 1 and 2, whereas P_1 and P_2 represent Törnqvist indexes for economies 1 and 2 measuring price changes from t to $t+1$.

Following Deaton (2012), we consider the change in PPP over time in natural logarithmic form. This is given by:

$$\ln PPP_2^{t+1} - \ln PPP_2^{t} = \frac{1}{2}\sum_{i=1}^{N}(e_{i1} + e_{i2})$$

$$\left[(\ln p_{i2}^{t+1} - \ln p_{i1}^{t+1}) - (\ln p_{i2}^{t} - \ln p_{i1}^{t})\right]$$

After simple rearrangement, it can be shown that:

$$\ln PPP_2^{t+1} - \ln PPP_2^{t} = \ln P_2 - \ln P_1$$

$$-\frac{1}{2}\sum_{i=1}^{N}(e_{i2} - e_{i1})\left[\ln\left(\frac{p_{i2}^{t+1}}{p_{i2}^{t}}\right) + \ln\left(\frac{p_{i1}^{t+1}}{p_{i1}^{t}}\right)\right]$$

Then, inconsistency between benchmarks and updates is given by:

$$\ln PPP_2^{t+1} - \ln PPP_2^{t} - (\ln P_2 - \ln P_1) =$$

$$-\frac{1}{2}\sum_{i=1}^{N}(e_{i2} - e_{i1})\left[\ln\left(\frac{p_{i2}^{t+1}}{p_{i2}^{t}}\right) + \ln\left(\frac{p_{i1}^{t+1}}{p_{i1}^{t}}\right)\right]$$

Deaton (2012) argues that this inconsistency depends on the covariance between differences in expenditure shares in the two economies and price movements in the two economies.

Inklaar and Rao (2019) conclude from the last expression on the right-hand side of the equation that the discrepancy between actual PPP in period $t+1$ for economy 2 and the extrapolated PPP from

period t using deflators will be equal to zero if prices of all commodities in economy 2 change by the same proportion, say α, and prices of all commodities in economy 1 also change by the same proportion, say β. The proportionate changes, α and β in the two economies, can be different. In this case, the inconsistency between the benchmark and extrapolation becomes:

$$\ln PPP_2^{t+1} - \ln PPP_2^{t} - (\ln P_2 - \ln P_1) =$$

$$-\frac{1}{2}\sum_{i=1}^{N}(e_{i2} - e_{i1})[\ln(\alpha) + \ln(\beta)] = 0$$

$$\text{since } \sum_{i=1}^{N} e_{i2} = \sum_{i=1}^{N} e_{i1} = 1$$

This condition, identified in Inklaar and Rao (2019), will not hold in general for all groups of commodities. Price changes for rice may differ from price changes for vegetables, etc. However, this condition is likely to hold at the level of the basic heading. In fact, one of the considerations in forming the basic headings is that each basic heading consists of items that are very similar and are therefore likely to exhibit similar price relativities and movements.

The main conclusion, and answer to the question regarding the level of aggregation at which extrapolation should be undertaken, is that extrapolation should occur at the level of the basic heading. This result formed the basis for the methodology proposed by Inklaar and Rao (2019) for constructing time series of PPPs and real expenditures for the years from 2012 to 2016, i.e., falling between the ICP's 2011 and 2017 cycles, where basic heading PPPs were first interpolated between benchmark years and subsequently aggregated using the prescribed GEKS procedure for estimating higher-level PPPs (World Bank 2020).

Option 5: Reduced Information Methods for Construction of Interim Updates

The need to explore shortcut methods to estimate PPPs for economies that do not participate in the ICP, along with the need to reduce the cost and burden of conducting ICP benchmark surveys by reducing the number of products to be priced, has been long recognized.

The first challenge of estimating PPPs for economies not participating in the ICP, and thereby extending comparisons across a larger number of economies, led to the pioneering work of Kravis, Heston, and Summers (1978) and ultimately to the publication of the Penn World Tables (Summers and Heston 1991; Feenstra et al. 2015). Much of the earlier work, as well as the recent method used by the World Bank, to fill gaps in PPPs for nonparticipating economies makes use of the regression relationship between price level, which is the ratio of PPPs to exchange rates and nominal or real GDP per capita or a range of other explanatory variables (Kravis and Lipsey 1983; Clague 1986, for example).

Meanwhile, research focusing on a reduction of the list of items to be priced has also received a lot of attention, largely due to the work of Ahmad (1980), whose study recognizes the challenge of a full ICP cycle and states:

> There are a number of drawbacks to the extensive projects such as the ICP. Unfortunately, they involve resources far beyond the capabilities of individual researchers. Further, they require the cooperation of many national organizations. Many countries do not have high levels of interests in this type of projects or sophisticated statistical organizations to undertake the work. Additionally, even for countries participating in such projects, their scope makes it impractical to produce full-scale comparisons for more than some benchmark years, perhaps every five or ten years. For intervening years, some simpler procedures must be adopted.

> Thus, for reasons of cost, lack of interest and expertise, and in order to fill the gaps in intra-benchmark years, shortcut methods or methods based on reduced information need to be found, methods that can duplicate the results of the ICP-type study, but which will not involve as much work and expense (Ahmad 1980, 4).

Ahmad investigated methods that might use reduced information as inputs, involving a fewer number of items in the basket of goods and services for which prices were to be collected. He first explored the possibility of using United Nations Post Adjustment[3] price data, collected typically for smaller baskets than those used in the ICP, and with prices collected from capital cities in different economies. After carefully establishing a mapping between United Nations and ICP categories, Ahmad found that "the category PPPs from the UN data were in general higher than those from the ICP data, and the magnitude of the difference had no clear cut pattern except that it varied a great deal from country to country" (Ahmad 1980, 19). Ahmad also explored the use of price data available from the United States Department of State for 16 economies, and came to a similar conclusion that these types of data cannot be used as reliable proxies for ICP data.

An alternative approach is to see if the data used in PPP compilation can be reduced without introducing systematic bias. Ahmad experimented with the idea of deleting categories (basic headings) whose weights were small. He considered three thresholds for selecting the most important categories: 75%, 50%, and 33% of all categories. Obviously, the ordering of the categories by expenditure shares depends on the choice of the economy selected for the ordering. Two options, one based on the average expenditure shares of three low-income economies (Colombia, India, and Kenya), and another based on the richest economy in the comparisons (the United States) were outlined. When the ratios of the actual PPPs to PPPs based on

---

truncated data were examined, it was found that the ratios tended to be become progressively smaller with the reduction in the sample size, instead of randomly distributed around 1. The conclusion drawn from this exercise is that: "This means that the more important a category is in consumer budgets, the lower the category prices are in most countries relative to the US. Therefore, reducing the sample size on the basis of expenditure weights will introduce a definite bias in the comparisons and consequently should be avoided" (Ahmad 1980, 29).

Another alternative method of reducing the number of products considered in Ahmad (1980) is to limit the number of products in each category to five, four, three, two, or one. This reduces the total number of products priced by 15%, 21%, 30%, 43%, and 70%, respectively. Obviously, these numbers depend on the actual price data from the ICP benchmarks used in Ahmad's study. The findings suggest that when the number of products is limited to five, the deviations from the actual are minimal, suggesting that five items in each list may be adequate. The main conclusion from this approach is that: "If it is necessary to operate on a reduced information basis, it is better to spread the risk by deleting items while retaining as many categories as possible than to pin hopes on a few categories found to be important in consumer budgets" (Ahmad 1980, 33).

The final option under the reduced information method explored in Ahmad (1980) is based on a regression approach and on the criterion of tracking observed PPPs with subsets of commodities. The approach described clearly recognizes the need to conduct regression for subgroups of products, instead of considering the full list of goods and services for calculating PPPs at the GDP level. Ahmad divided household consumption into three groups: (i) food, beverages, and tobacco; (ii) clothing, furnishing, and other (other than what is covered in the first and third groups); and (iii) rent, medical care, transport, and recreation and education. For the remaining sectors, the following groups were considered: (i) producer durables, (ii) construction, and (iii) government. Data from the ICP's 1973 cycle were used in implementing the procedure.

Ahmad summarized the results as: "The six sectoral equations required a total of 46 item prices (some of the items were used in more than one sector). These items and the associated regressions constituted the core of the reduced information procedure. The $\bar{R}^2$ of these regressions were mostly above 0.99, and the maximum residuals for any country were no more than 3.8%. Consequently, this procedure replicated the 1973 comparisons almost perfectly" (Ahmad 1980, 49).

In summary, the idea of identifying a subsample of items for price collection was first proposed and implemented in Ahmad's seminal 1980 study. While the general criterion for selecting the size of the subsample, and exactly which products will be included in it, has been one of tracking the observed PPPs as closely as possible, the methods employed differ significantly and each of them is likely to produce a slightly different outcome.

This research study on the compilation of PPPs for 2016 builds on the notion of the reduced information approach and on the feasibility of identifying such a subsample of products for price collection. It continues the work of ADB's 2009 update study into identifying the best subsample of goods and services to be priced. This procedure known as the "Core List Approach" is described in detail in Chapter 4.

4. Methodology and Survey Framework for the Research Study

The main objective of this research study on 2016 data was similar to that of the Asian Development Bank (ADB) study conducted in 2009 (ADB 2012a), i.e., to explore an alternative approach for estimating purchasing power parities (PPPs) in the years between the benchmark cycles of the International Comparison Program (ICP); an approach that might be less resource intensive than a regular ICP cycle.

In particular, the study aimed to provide more firmly based regional price and volume comparisons of gross domestic product (GDP) and its major component expenditures for the year 2016, compared to what could be obtained by the conventional method of extrapolating PPPs from the ICP's 2011 benchmark cycle. The study also explores the potential to provide PPPs for a larger number of expenditure aggregates, unlike the conventional extrapolation methodology currently used to derive PPPs at the level of GDP and household consumption.

To meet the objectives of the study and estimate PPPs for 2016 using the reduced information approach, the following procedures were implemented to reduce the burden of data collection for the prices of household products:

(i) A core list of household consumption products (core product list)—a subset of the full household product list used in the ICP's 2011 cycle in Asia and the Pacific—was identified for pricing in 2016. This reduced the number of items to be priced in 2016 to less than two-fifths of the original 2011 list.

(ii) To further reduce the burden of price surveys, price data for the core product list was collected only in capital cities in 2016. In order to meet the requirement that prices must be nationally representative, a set of adjustment factors—ratios of capital-city average price to national level average price for each individual item priced in 2011—were used to adjust capital-city average prices to national annual average prices at the item level for 2016.

(iii) The frequency of collecting prices for household shop items was minimized to once every quarter, although some participating economies collected prices for certain categories of products on a monthly basis.

(iv) Finally, basic-heading level PPPs were generated using the price data collected in 2016 for core product list. Adjustment factors—ratios of PPPs calculated from the core product list and PPPs from the full 2011 product list—were established for each basic heading to adjust the 2016 basic-heading PPPs generated from the core product list.

Building the Core Product List

The core product list or core list is the optimal subset of the full product list or full list used in the ICP's 2011 benchmark cycle. The core list was compiled specifically for the purpose of calculating PPPs and real expenditures for 2016, reducing the resources needed to collect prices for a full product list as practiced in an ICP benchmark cycle. The selection of items in the core product list was determined separately for each basic heading. This is because the ICP's basic headings are the building blocks from which higher-level aggregates are derived. This approach is supported by Ahmad (1980), where the best subset of products is determined using a regression approach at the category level. This is also in line with the guidance of Inklaar and Rao (2017) regarding the optimal level of disaggregation for extrapolation of PPPs, where it is considered best if the extrapolation is undertaken at the level of the basic headings. Furthermore, the approach used in this study on 2016 data is consistent with the one used in the similar study conducted by ADB in 2009.

Basic Principle for Determining the Subset of Core Products

The main principle for determining the subset of products to be selected under each basic heading was the same as followed for the 2009 update study. The principle followed in this study is that the products identified for inclusion in the core product list under each basic heading should result in PPPs for the basic headings that deviate the least from the PPPs calculated using the full product list. The core product list was therefore identified using the actual price data collected for the full list in the ICP's 2011 benchmark year. The best subset is the core list of a given size that minimizes the root mean square error (RMSE) of the core-list-based PPPs from the full-list-based PPPs calculated across all the participating economies.

This criterion, as applied to any selected basic heading, is as follows: Let PPP_j^{Full} and PPP_j^{Core} be the PPPs for economy j, calculated using, respectively, the full and core list of products among a set of M economies. As per standard practice, the PPP for Hong Kong, China (the reference economy) is set to 1 in both sets of PPPs. The PPPs based on the full sample here, $\{PPP_j^{Full}, j = 1,2,\ldots,M\}$ refer to the actual PPPs for the basic heading from the ICP's 2011 benchmark year.

The objective is to select the core list of products that ensure PPP_j^{Core} deviates the least from PPP_j^{Full} or, equally, the ratio $\frac{PPP_j^{Core}}{PPP_j^{Full}}$ is as close to 1 as possible. For any given subset of products included in the core, it is possible to calculate the RMSE defined by:

$$RMSE^{Core} = \sqrt{\frac{1}{M}\sum_{j=1}^{M}\left[\frac{PPP_j^{Core}}{PPP_j^{Full}} - 1\right]^2}$$

The basic idea is that, for all feasible subsets of core products of the given size, $RMSE^{Core}$ is calculated, then the core products comprising the subset that minimizes the RMSE are considered the "optimal" or "selected" core products for that basic heading.

The procedure described above is well designed and serves the main purpose of identifying the core list of items. However, this procedure is not invariant to the choice of the reference economy as the RMSE defined would have the PPPs for Hong Kong, China equal to 1 for both the full and core list of products. In order to make it base invariant, the PPPs are normalized to the geometric mean of PPPs of all participating economies. Let the geometric means be denoted, respectively, by $PPP^{Core,GM}$ and $PPP^{Full,GM}$, then the normalized RMSE invariant to the choice of the base or reference economy or RMSE^{Core,*} is given by:

$$RMSE^{Core,*} = \sqrt{\frac{1}{M}\sum_{j=1}^{M}\left[\frac{\frac{PPP_j^{Core}}{PPP^{Core,GM}}}{\frac{PPP_j^{Full}}{PPP^{Full,GM}}} - 1\right]^2}$$

This is the criterion applied in the 2009 study in the selection of the best subset of products to be included in the core product list.

An Illustrative Example of the Combinatorial Approach to Product Selection: "Rice" Basic Heading

The following steps were used in identifying the core list of products to be sampled for this research study on 2016 data. The steps were implemented for each basic heading separately, but the discussion here illustrates the selected basic heading, "Rice". The "Rice" basic heading consists of 20 different items of rice in the ICP's 2011 cycle household product list in Asia and the Pacific. As is usually the case, not all rice items were priced by all economies in the region. In Table 4.1, cells marked with "X" identify the products for which average prices were submitted by the 20 economies (denoted by letters A to T) in the "Rice" basic heading in the ICP's 2011 cycle which are covered in this study. The "-" symbol indicates that the item was not priced by that particular economy.

Column 3 of Table 4.1 shows the number of economies that priced a particular item. "White rice #3" and "Premium rice #2" were two of the most-priced items, each priced by 14 of the 20 economies that participated in the ICP's 2011 cycle in Asia and the Pacific and are

also part of this research study. On the other hand, "Coarse rice #2" and "Coarse rice #3" were the least-priced items, each priced by only three economies.

This research study employs the same combinatorial approach used in the 2009 study to select a subset of items or 'core list' in each basic heading (ADB 2012a, p. 17). This combinatorial approach is applied only after the size of the core list is determined. Suppose the size of the core list is set at six items for the "Rice" basic heading shown in Table 4.1. This means that the core list is about 30% of the full list, which comprises 20 items. The question here is: "Which six of the

Table 4.1: Full List of Items Priced Under "Rice" Basic Heading by Economy, 2011

Item Code	Item Description	Number of Economies Pricing the Item	CV^a	2011 Rice Items Priced																			
				A	B	C	D	E	F	G	H	I	J	K	L	M	N	O	P	Q	R	S	T
(1)	(2)	(3)	(4)	(5)	(6)	(7)	(8)	(9)	(10)	(11)	(12)	(13)	(14)	(15)	(16)	(17)	(18)	(19)	(20)	(21)	(22)	(23)	(24)
1101111011	Coarse rice #3	3	0.38	-	-	-	-	X	X	-	-	-	-	-	-	-	-	-	-	-	X	-	-
11011110110	White rice #3	14	0.25	-	X	-	-	X	X	X	-	X	X	X	X	X	X	X	-	X	X	-	X
11011110111	White rice #4	6	0.14	-	-	-	-	X	X	X	-	X	-	X	-	X	-	-	-	-	-	-	-
11011110112	White rice #5	7	0.22	-	-	-	-	-	X	X	-	X	X	X	-	X	-	X	-	-	-	-	-
11011110113	White rice #6	5	0.30	-	-	-	-	X	-	X	-	-	X	X	-	X	-	-	-	-	-	-	-
11011110114	White rice #7	6	0.32	X	-	-	-	X	-	X	-	X	-	X	-	-	-	-	-	-	X	-	-
11011110115	White rice #8	8	0.20	X	-	-	-	X	-	X	-	X	-	-	-	-	X	-	X	-	X	X	-
11011110116	White rice #9	6	0.41	X	-	X	X	X	-	X	-	X	-	-	-	-	-	-	-	-	-	-	-
11011110117	White rice #10	9	0.26	X	-	X	X	X	-	X	-	X	X	-	-	-	-	X	-	X	-	-	-
11011110118	Premium rice #1	8	0.21	X	-	-	-	X	X	X	-	X	-	-	X	-	X	-	-	-	X	-	-
11011110119	Premium rice #2	14	0.27	X	-	X	X	X	-	X	-	X	X	X	X	-	X	-	-	X	X	X	X
11011110120	Premium rice #3	6	0.33	-	-	-	X	X	-	X	-	X	-	-	X	-	-	X	-	-	-	-	-
11011110121	Premium rice #4	12	0.22	X	X	X	-	X	-	X	-	X	X	X	-	-	X	-	X	X	-	-	X
1101111013	Coarse rice #2	3	0.56	-	-	-	-	X	-	X	-	X	-	-	-	-	-	-	-	-	-	-	-
1101111014	Coarse rice #6	4	0.20	-	-	-	-	X	-	X	-	-	X	-	X	-	-	-	-	-	-	-	-
1101111015	Coarse rice #5	5	0.18	-	-	-	-	X	-	X	-	X	-	X	-	X	-	-	-	-	-	-	-
1101111017	Brown rice	12	0.45	-	-	X	X	X	X	X	X	-	-	X	X	-	X	X	-	X	X	-	-
1101111018	White rice #1	13	0.32	-	-	-	X	X	X	X	-	X	-	X	X	X	-	X	X	X	-	X	X
1101111019	White rice #2	9	0.31	-	-	-	-	X	-	X	-	X	-	X	X	-	-	-	X	-	X	X	X
11011110201	Glutinous rice	11	0.34	-	X	X	X	-	-	X	-	-	-	-	X	X	X	X	-	X	X	-	X
CV of CPD residuals by economy				0.11	2.24	1.30	0.03	0.04	0.04	0.07	-	0.02	0.01	0.03	0.00	0.00	0.03	0.00	0.69	0.00	0.36	0.00	0.04
Number of items priced by economy				7	3	6	7	18	7	19	1	15	7	11	8	9	7	7	3	9	6	5	6

0.00 = magnitude is less than half of unit employed, CPD = country-product-dummy, CV = coefficient of variation.
Note: "X" corresponds to a product priced while "–" corresponds to a product not priced in the 2011 International Comparison Program.
^a Coefficients of variation of prices.
Source: Asian Development Bank estimates.

20 items should be selected?" One approach would be to choose six items at random from the list of 20 items. However, if the items were randomly selected, there would be no guarantee about the quality of the outcome and, each time a random sample of six items was drawn, a completely different set of PPPs for the basic heading across economies would result. A criterion to choose between all possible samples is therefore needed, and it is here that the combinatorial approach provides a solution. The number of different subsets of six items out of 20 can be calculated using the standard combinatorial formula:

$$_{20}C_6 = \frac{20!}{6!(20-6)!} \text{ wherein } n! = 1 \times 2 \times 3 \times \ldots \times n$$

In the case of the "Rice" basic heading, the number of different subsets of six items drawn out of the full list of 20 is 38,760. The problem then is selecting one of these 38,760 possible subsets for the purpose of calculating the PPPs for this basic heading. Since PPPs need to be calculated using price data for any selected core list of six products, not all selected subsets are feasible in the sense that, for some selections, it would not be possible to calculate PPPs for all the economies in the Asia and Pacific region using the data in Table 4.1. For example, presume the selected subset is the first six items listed in Table 4.1: Coarse rice #3;

White rice #3; White rice #4; White rice #5; White rice #6; and White rice #7. For this selection, no 2011 price data are available for any of these products from economies A, C, D, H, and P. This means that PPPs for this basic heading cannot be calculated for all economies for this subset of six items. Therefore, only those subsets that are feasible were considered in this study.

The next question is: "How does one select from the set of feasible core lists?" This is where the RMSE criterion becomes relevant. For every selection of six items, the RMSE can be calculated to identify the subset that gives the lowest value of the RMSE denoted by $RMSE_6^*$—the RMSE associated with the optimal or best subset of items in the core size of six. In the case of the "Rice" basic heading, this criterion leads to the subset of six items shown in Table 4.2 (from the items in Table 4.1). Based on these ratios, the RMSE associated with the optimum selection is 7.2%.

Some interesting features of the *optimal core list* for the "Rice" basic heading may be noted. For example, while it can be seen from Table 4.1 that "White rice #1" was priced by 13 economies in 2011, the product was not included in this core list, whereas "White rice #8" and "White rice #2," which were priced by only eight and nine economies, respectively, were selected.

Table 4.2: Core List of Rice Items Priced by Economy, 2016

Item Code	Item Description	Number of Economies Pricing the Item	A	B	C	D	E	F	G	H	I	J	K	L	M	N	O	P	Q	R	S	T
(1)	(2)	(3)	(4)	(5)	(6)	(7)	(8)	(9)	(10)	(11)	(12)	(13)	(14)	(15)	(16)	(17)	(18)	(19)	(20)	(21)	(22)	(23)
11011110110	White rice #3	15	–	X	–	–	X	X	X	–	X	X	X	X	X	X	X	X	X	X	–	X
11011110115	White rice #8	9	X	–	–	–	X	–	X	–	X	–	–	–	–	X	–	X	–	X	X	X
11011110119	Premium rice #2	15	X	–	X	X	X	X	X	–	X	X	X	X	–	X	–	–	X	X	X	X
1101111017	Brown rice	13	–	–	X	X	X	X	X	X	–	–	X	X	–	X	X	–	X	X	–	X
1101111019	White rice #2	10	–	–	–	–	X	X	X	–	X	–	X	X	X	–	–	–	X	–	X	X
11011110201	Glutinous rice	11	–	X	X	X	–	–	X	–	–	–	–	X	X	X	X	–	X	X	–	X

Note: "X" corresponds to a product priced while "–" corresponds to a product not priced in the 2016 Purchasing Power Parity research study.
Source: Asian Development Bank estimates.

Size of the Core Product List

The selection of core products using the combinatorial approach depends on what proportion of the full product list is to be priced. A general rule to select a core list comprising 30% of the items from the full product list under each basic heading was applied for the 2009 research study. This 30% ratio was identified by examining the trade-off between the reduction in the RMSE and the cost of sampling. The RMSE reduces to zero when the core list includes all the items in the basic heading list—in which case there is no reduced information in the alternative approach. Similarly, if the number of products included in the core list is very small, the cost of sampling and surveys would be significantly reduced, but the RMSE would be high. It should be noted that the RMSE is a decreasing function of the size of the core product list.

For this study based on 2016 data, as in the case of the 2009 study, a target of 30% was agreed as a general principle. The starting point in identifying the core list, therefore, was to target price collection for about 30% of the full product list applied to each basic heading in the ICP's 2011 cycle. In addition to the 30% ratio, a second criterion was that the core products selected within each basic heading should produce an RMSE of below 15%, based on the full 2011 list. The outcome of applying these criteria was that, in some cases, more than 30% could be selected in a basic heading. Further, for some basic headings in which only a few products were specified in 2011, or basic headings with only one or two items, all items were included in the core list.

The above processes resulted in the selection of an optimal subset of household products for each basic heading from the ICP's 2011 benchmark, for which prices were collected in 2016. It should be noted that, for this research study, a core product list following the above approach was prepared only for the survey of household products, which is the most resource-intensive survey in a benchmark ICP cycle. For nonhousehold products, the price surveys in 2016 were carried out using the full product list, as was the case in the ICP's 2011 cycle.

Using the Core List to Estimate Purchasing Power Parities in 2016

Once the core list of products was determined for each basic heading, these lists were used by the participating economies to conduct price surveys in 2016 and provide the average prices for the products listed. However, since the calculations used products priced only from the core list, the resulting PPPs are expected to be different from the PPPs that would have been derived from the full list. In view of this, adjustment factors for the basic heading PPPs of 2016, calculated using the core list specific to each economy, were derived from the price data for core and full lists in the ICP's 2011 benchmark year.

For 2011, PPPs from the full list were already available for the basic headings that were priced[1]. In addition, PPPs for 2011 from the core list could be calculated using the prices of the items in the core list. Based on these two sets of PPPs, the adjustment ratio from core-to-full item list was calculated for each basic heading for each economy as:

$$ADJ_j^{Rice} = \frac{PPP_j^{Rice,Core}}{PPP_j^{Rice,Full}} \text{ for } j = 1,2,\dots,20 \text{ and } ADJ_{HKG}^{Rice} = 1$$

To see how the adjustment factors would compare with Asia and the Pacific, the PPPs were normalized by dividing with the geometric mean of PPPs for all economies. Table 4.3 shows the adjustment factors for the "Rice" basic heading. These adjustment factors were calculated by dividing the normalized PPP for the core list of the "Rice" basic heading by the normalized PPPs for the full list of the "Rice" basic

---

[1]   Prices are not collected for all basic headings. For some basic headings where it is difficult to price items following the conventional approach, reference PPPs from one or more related basic headings are used as reference.

Table 4.3: Core List to Full List Adjustment Factors for "Rice" Basic Heading from 2011 International Comparison Program by Economy[a]
(Asia and the Pacific=1.00)

Basic Heading Code	Basic Heading Description	BAN	BHU	BRU	CAM	FIJ	HKG	IND	INO	LAO	MAL	MLD	MON	NEP	PAK	PHI	SIN	SRI	TAP	THA	VIE
(1)	(2)	(3)	(4)	(5)	(6)	(7)	(8)	(9)	(10)	(11)	(12)	(13)	(14)	(15)	(16)	(17)	(18)	(19)	(20)	(21)	(22)
1101111	Rice	0.97	1.22	0.96	1.04	1.00	0.97	1.03	1.03	0.92	0.96	1.02	0.95	0.93	0.96	1.08	1.09	0.89	0.95	1.04	1.04

BAN = Bangladesh; BHU = Bhutan; BRU = Brunei Darussalam; CAM = Cambodia; FIJ = Fiji; HKG = Hong Kong, China; IND = India; INO = Indonesia; LAO = Lao People's Democratic Republic; MAL = Malaysia; MLD = Maldives; MON = Mongolia; NEP = Nepal; PAK = Pakistan; PHI = Philippines; SIN = Singapore; SRI = Sri Lanka; TAP = Taipei,China; THA = Thailand; VIE = Viet Nam.
[a] The 2011 International Comparison Program data were used to estimate adjustment factors or the ratios of the purchasing power parity (PPP) of the core and the full list for each basic heading. Adjustment factors were derived for each basic heading and used to adjust the basic heading PPPs derived for 2016 from the prices of core list to adjust to full list PPPs.
Source: Asian Development Bank estimates.

heading, using price data submitted by the economies that participated in both the ICP's 2011 cycle and this research study.

If the adjustment factor is 0.97 for an economy, e.g., Bangladesh, the PPP obtained using the core product list in 2016 is adjusted to the full product list by dividing it by 0.97. The implicit assumption in this adjustment mechanism is that ratios obtained for 2011 continued to apply for 2016. The adjustment factors were calculated for each basic heading for household consumption from the ICP's 2011 price data. The adjustment factors were above 1 for some economies and below 1 for others. In the case of the "Rice" basic heading, the range of adjustment factors was in a narrow band from 0.89 to 1.22.

However, these ratios exhibited different patterns for different basic headings. In most basic headings the adjustment factors ranged from below 1.00 to above 1.00, indicating that, within the same basic heading, in some economies the PPPs based on core list alone understated the PPPs, while in some others it overstated the PPP. In a few basic headings, all the adjustment factors were below 1—meaning that the use of the core list of items only understated the PPPs for all economies. In very few cases, all adjustment factors were above 1.00, indicating that the use of only the core list overstated PPPs. This variability in adjustment factors for different basic headings suggests that it is important to implement core-to-full list adjustments when implementing the reduced information approach based on the core lists identified using the combinatorial approach.

Survey Framework and Coverage for Data Collection in 2016

The survey framework for this research study was designed to cover all main aggregates making up GDP. Thus, the scope of price surveys extended to household products for *individual consumption expenditure by households*; government compensation for *government consumption expenditure*; and machinery and equipment, and construction, for *gross fixed capital formation*—as was the case in the ICP's 2011 benchmark cycle. However, coverage of price surveys varied according to the aggregate under consideration.

Table 4.4 shows the total number of items in the product lists for which price data were collected in the ICP's 2011 cycle and in this study for estimating the PPPs and real expenditures for GDP and its major aggregates in 2016. Column 4 of Table 4.4 shows that, in the 2011 cycle, prices for 1,190 products were collected, of which the biggest share (923 items or 78%) was for household products, with the remaining 22% of surveyed prices covering nonhousehold products. Columns 5 to 8 of Table 4.4 show the total number of items in the final list for the 2016 price surveys. This includes the list of core products selected using the combinatorial approach (Column 6) as well as "fast evolving" (Column 8) and "core and fast evolving" items (Column 7). The items under the "fast evolving" column are newly added items. Most of the fast-evolving products are in the transport, communication, and recreation and culture GDP components.

Table 4.4: Gross Domestic Product and Its Structures: Number of Basic Headings and Items Priced in Asia and the Pacific, 2011 and 2016

			Number of Items				
				2016			
Category	Components	Number of Basic Headings	2011[a]	Total	Core	Core and Fast evolving	Fast evolving
(1)	(2)	(3)	(4)	(5)	(6)	(7)	(8)
Gross Domestic Product	a+r+s+t+u	155	1,190	638	578	16	44
Actual individual consumption by households	a = b+p+q	136	938	403	343	16	44
Individual consumption expenditure by households	b = Σ(c to o)	110	923	390	330	16	44
Food and nonalcoholic beverages	c	29	258	124	124	–	–
Alcoholic beverages, tobacco, and narcotics	d	5	24	20	20	–	–
Clothing and footwear	e	5	96	33	33	–	–
Housing, water, electricity, gas, and other fuels	f	8	14	12	12	–	–
Furnishings, household equipment, and routine maintenance of the house	g	13	121	38	29	9	–
Health[b]	h	7	155	26	26	–	–
Transport	i	13	65	42	23	2	17
Communication	j	3	18	14	6	1	7
Recreation and culture	k	13	91	53	29	4	20
Education	l	1	6	2	2	–	–
Restaurants and hotels	m	2	21	9	9	–	–
Miscellaneous goods and services	n	10	54	17	17	–	–
Net expenditures of residents abroad	o	1	c	c	c	c	c
Individual consumption expenditure by NPISHs	p	5	c	c	c	c	c
Individual consumption expenditure by government	q	21	15	13	13	–	–
Collective consumption expenditure by government	r	5	29	20	20	–	–
Gross fixed capital formation	s	10	223	215	215	–	–
Changes in inventories and acquisitions less disposals of valuables	t	2	c	c	c	c	c
Balance of exports and imports	u	2	c	c	c	c	c

– = magnitude equals zero, NPISHs = nonprofit institutions serving households.
Note: 2011 refers to the 2011 International Comparison Program and 2016 refers to the 2016 purchasing power parity research study.
[a] Number of items are different from the 2011 International Comparison Program report due to changes in the classification.
[b] Number of products includes split items for pharmaceutical products.
[c] Reference purchasing power parities were used.
Source: Asian Development Bank estimates.

The "core and fast evolving" items are those that belong to the core list drawn from the ICP's 2011 list, but the specifications and brands may have changed from 2011 to 2016. Those basic headings marked with "c" are basic headings for which reference PPPs were used (Appendix 2).

As outlined in the previous section, the core product list for household products for 2016 was a subset of the ICP's full product list for 2011, selected using a combinatorial approach. The product lists for government compensation (used for measuring individual and collective consumption expenditure of the government), machinery and equipment, and construction in 2016 are almost the same as those used in 2011, with some minor changes. For the nonhousehold products priced in 2016, the core lists represented the full lists of products as would be included in a usual ICP cycle benchmark.

Household and Nonhousehold Surveys: Product Lists and Survey Coverage

The standard ICP practice is to first determine the product lists to be priced. It further requires statisticians to determine the scope of price collection surveys in terms of the geographical coverage needed to collect prices that are representative of the underlying goods and services included in the valuation of GDP and its component aggregates. Once the product list is finalized, prices are normally collected by the participating economies using a survey framework that results in annual national average prices. Table 4.5 describes in brief the scope and price survey framework for each of the main aggregates of GDP for this research study on 2016 data in comparison with the ICP's 2011 benchmark cycle.

The study's approach to developing price lists and survey coverage for household consumption, government compensation, machinery and equipment, and construction was as follows.

Household consumption. The price survey of household products for *individual consumption expenditure by households* in the ICP's 2011 cycle comprised almost 80% of the products for which data were collected. The household products survey was the main vehicle in which the reduced information approach was applied in this research study.

The basic approach adopted, as was the case in the 2009 study, was to reduce the burden of price collection on the participating economies, instead relying on prices collected for a reduced list of products. In general, 30% of the ICP's 2011 full product list was considered the baseline for reducing the number of items to be sampled in 2016. However, this principle had to be relaxed in the case of those basic headings that included only a few items. Further, the combinatorial approach was mainly

Table 4.5: Scope and Coverage of Price Surveys in Asia and the Pacific, 2011 and 2016

Price Survey	2011	2016
Individual consumption expenditure by households	Items: Price collection covered 923 items in the list for Asia and the Pacific. The 2011 list was based on the 2005 and 2009 product lists, with obsolete items dropped and new items added based on regional updates and updates from global core list for 2011.	Items: Price collection covered 346 (about 37%) items of the 923 items included in the 2011 full list and supplemented with 44 fast-evolving items, resulting in 390 items.
	Coverage: Nationwide	Coverage: Capital cities[a]
	Frequency: Monthly and quarterly for most items. Weekly for fruits and vegetables. For less volatile items, such as utilities, semiannually or annually.	Frequency: Monthly or quarterly depending upon the price variability and as decided by each participating economy. For less volatile items, such as utilities, semiannually or annually.
Government final consumption expenditure	Items: Price collection included average compensation for 44 government occupations; 38 occupations were included in the PPP calculation, as approved by the Regional Advisory Board for ICP's 2011 cycle in Asia and the Pacific.	Same as 2011 but excluding those not in the global list, reducing to 33 government posts.
	Coverage: Nationwide	Coverage: Nationwide
	Frequency: One-time collection from administrative records	Frequency: One-time collection from administrative records
Gross fixed capital formation in construction	Items: Price collection covered 46 global construction input items relevant to Asia and the Pacific and used relevance indicators. Reference PPPs were used from aggregate machinery and equipment for PPPs for rental equipment.	Items: Price collection included annual average prices for regionally relevant 54 items of construction input items of materials, equipment rental, and labor; regional relevance indicators were also used.
	Coverage: Capital cities	Coverage: Capital cities
	Frequency: One-time price collection	Frequency: One-time price collection
Gross fixed capital formation in machinery and equipment	Items: Price collection covered 177 global items relevant to Asia and the Pacific.	Items: Price collection included annual average prices for 161 items including other products.
	Coverage: Capital cities	Coverage: Capital cities
	Frequency: One-time price collection	Frequency: One-time price collection

ICP = International Comparison Program, PPP = purchasing power parity.

[a] The prices for household core products were collected in capital cities only except for Cambodia, India, and Pakistan where prices were collected in some major cities including the capital city and were adjusted to obtain national prices accordingly.

Note: 2011 refers to the 2011 International Comparison Program and 2016 refers to the 2016 purchasing power parity research study.

Source: Asian Development Bank.

used for selecting the core product lists of household consumption for each basic heading. This approach resulted in the selection of 346 core products (nearly 37%) of the 923 products included in the ICP's 2011 full product list. The core product lists were supplemented by an additional 44 fast-evolving items, taking the total to 390 household products to be priced in 2016.

This approach required the 2016 PPPs for household consumption to be derived from the prices of core-list products to be adjusted as if prices for all items in the full list were collected. Table 4.6 shows the number of items selected for pricing under each basic heading of household consumption in both the ICP's 2011 cycle and in 2016.

Columns 3 and 4 of Table 4.6 show, respectively, the number of items priced in 2011 and the number of items selected in the core list using the combinatorial approach for 2016. Column 5 shows the ratio of the 2011 items included in the core list for 2016, arranged by basic headings. From this column, it is clear that there are a number of basic headings for which the ratio is well above 30%, while for several basic headings the ratio is equal to 100%. The percentage of core items in 2016 relative to 2011 for the whole of household consumption is 37%. Columns 6 to 25 show the number of items priced by each of the 20 participating economies, after the capital-to-national adjustment and exclusion of outlier prices, arranged by basic headings.

In order to reduce the burden of price collection, this research study relied on price data collected only from capital cities in the participating economies. This approach of collecting only capital-city prices required adjusting those prices to average prices at the national level.

Finally, prices were collected with quarterly or monthly frequency, depending on the variability in the prices of the items, as decided by the individual participating economies.

Government compensation. Data for government compensation were collected for 33 government occupations in 2016 representing a range of collective and individual government services. The participating economies submitted average compensation data for each of these government occupations. Total compensation included: (i) basic pay, (ii) allowances and other additional payments, (iii) employer's social security contributions, and (iv) in-kind remuneration. As government compensation data for selected occupations represented the prices for government services, no further adjustments were required. Adjustments were, however, introduced for differences in productivity across economies, following a similar method that was applied for the revised results of the ICP's 2011 cycle and for the 2017 cycle (ADB 2020).[2]

Machinery and equipment. The survey covering machinery and equipment entailed one-time data collection to obtain national average prices for 161 items. No adjustments were needed for the machinery and equipment PPPs as the survey's geographical coverage and the methodology was the same as for the ICP's 2011 cycle.

Construction. In the case of construction, one-time data collection was conducted to obtain national prices for 54 input items. Aside from prices of input items, economies were also asked to provide information on "resource mix" in the form of shares of main inputs (materials, equipment rental, and labor). The "relevance" criterion was applied to the inclusion of certain types of inputs in different types of construction. For example, equipment rental was not included in residential construction, but input costs of equipment rental in civil engineering and nonresidential construction may be substantial. No adjustments were needed for the construction PPPs as the survey's geographical coverage and the methodology was the same as for the ICP's 2011 cycle.

---

2   Thailand was unable to provide complete data on compensation of employees as per the ICP's technical and conceptual requirements. Government compensation data of Thailand for 2016 were estimated by extrapolating government compensation data for 2011, with the deflator of government final consumption expenditure, as was done for the ICP's 2017 cycle, to fill the data gap for Thailand.

Table 4.6: Number of Items Priced by Basic Heading in Household Consumption and by Economy, 2011 and 2016ª

Basic Heading Code	Basic Heading Description	Number of Items specified		Ratio 2016 to 2011	Number of Household Consumption items Priced in 2016																				
		2011	2016b		BAN	BHU	BRU	CAM	FIJ	HKG	IND	INO	LAO	MAL	MLD	MON	NEP	PAK	PHI	SIN	SRI	TAP	THA	VIE
(1)	(2)	(3)	(4)	(5)	(6)	(7)	(8)	(9)	(10)	(11)	(12)	(13)	(14)	(15)	(16)	(17)	(18)	(19)	(20)	(21)	(22)	(23)	(24)	(25)
1101111	Rice	20	6	0.30	3	2	2	5	–	2	4	4	3	4	1	1	4	2	4	3	4	3	5	3
1101112	Other cereals, flour and other cereal products	18	6	0.33	4	3	4	2	2	4	4	1	2	4	2	3	5	3	3	3	3	4	2	3
1101113	Bread	6	6	1.00	2	–	5	5	5	4	4	5	3	2	2	4	2	1	4	3	4	3	6	5
1101114	Other bakery products	11	3	0.27	3	1	3	2	2	1	2	–	1	1	1	–	2	2	2	1	3	2	3	2
1101115	Pasta products and couscous	7	2	0.29	1	1	1	1	1	2	1	–	1	1	1	2	2	2	2	2	1	2	–	2
1101121	Beef and veal	14	3	0.21	3	1	2	2	3	2	3	3	3	2	1	3	–	2	3	3	–	2	3	2
1101122	Pork	7	2	0.29	–	–	–	2	1	2	2	1	1	2	–	1	1	–	2	2	–	2	2	2
1101123	Lamb, mutton and goat	6	1	0.17	–	–	–	–	1	1	1	–	–	1	–	1	1	1	–	1	1	1	–	–
1101124	Poultry	11	3	0.27	3	2	2	3	2	2	3	2	2	3	2	1	1	3	2	3	1	2	2	3
1101125	Other meats and meat preparations	7	4	0.57	2	2	2	3	2	3	3	1	1	1	1	1	1	1	4	3	3	2	3	3
1101131	Fresh, chilled, or frozen fish and seafood	17	5	0.29	2	1	4	2	2	4	4	4	3	3	2	–	1	2	4	3	3	3	3	4
1101132	Preserved or processed fish and seafood	7	7	1.00	2	2	7	5	2	3	4	5	3	2	3	2	1	–	5	6	3	5	6	4
1101141	Fresh milk	4	4	1.00	2	3	1	1	1	1	4	1	2	–	–	2	3	3	2	1	1	1	1	1
1101142	Preserved milk and other milk products	10	3	0.30	3	2	3	2	1	3	1	3	2	2	1	1	1	3	3	3	1	3	2	2
1101143	Cheese and curd	7	7	1.00	1	2	5	2	1	3	4	4	–	2	2	4	4	3	3	4	3	4	1	2
1101144	Eggs and egg-based products	4	4	1.00	3	1	2	4	1	3	4	4	1	1	1	3	2	2	4	4	3	4	3	4
1101151	Butter and margarine	5	2	0.40	2	–	1	1	1	–	1	–	1	2	–	–	1	2	1	1	2	1	1	–
1101153	Other edible oils and fats	9	3	0.33	3	1	3	3	1	2	3	3	1	1	2	2	1	3	3	3	3	3	3	1
1101161	Fresh or chilled fruit	12	4	0.33	2	3	4	3	3	4	4	1	2	2	1	4	2	3	4	4	3	3	3	3
1101162	Frozen, preserved, or processed fruit and fruit-based products	4	4	1.00	1	–	2	2	1	1	3	1	–	3	–	1	2	1	2	4	1	3	2	1
1101171	Fresh or chilled vegetables, other than potatoes and other tuber vegetables	15	5	0.33	5	3	4	5	2	5	3	3	3	2	1	2	3	3	3	5	3	5	3	3
1101172	Fresh or chilled potatoes and other tuber vegetables	4	4	1.00	3	–	2	4	3	3	4	1	2	4	1	2	1	2	3	3	3	3	3	3
1101173	Frozen, preserved, or processed vegetables and vegetable–based products	10	7	0.70	5	2	5	6	2	5	6	3	3	5	4	3	5	5	4	5	6	5	4	6
1101181	Sugar	3	3	1.00	2	1	2	2	1	2	3	1	2	2	–	2	1	1	2	2	2	3	3	3
1101182	Jams, marmalades, and honey	3	3	1.00	3	1	2	2	3	2	2	1	2	3	2	3	3	1	2	3	2	3	2	2
1101183	Confectionery, chocolate, and ice cream	6	6	1.00	4	–	6	4	2	6	2	3	2	3	4	4	4	3	3	3	1	5	6	4
1101191	Food products n.e.c.	13	4	0.31	1	2	3	3	–	2	1	3	1	2	–	1	3	1	2	4	1	2	4	3

continued on next page

Table 4.6 continued

Basic Heading Code (1)	Basic Heading Description (2)	Number of Items specified 2011 (3)	2016[b] (4)	Ratio 2016 to 2011 (5)	Number of Household Consumption items Priced in 2016																				
					BAN (6)	BHU (7)	BRU (8)	CAM (9)	FIJ (10)	HKG (11)	IND (12)	INO (13)	LAO (14)	MAL (15)	MLD (16)	MON (17)	NEP (18)	PAK (19)	PHI (20)	SIN (21)	SRI (22)	TAP (23)	THA (24)	VIE (25)
1101211	Coffee, tea, and cocoa	15	5	0.33	5	–	2	2	3	4	2	3	2	2	1	2	2	4	2	4	3	2	3	1
1101221	Mineral waters, soft drinks, fruit and vegetable juices	8	8	1.00	8	7	5	6	5	6	7	5	3	4	2	6	8	6	4	7	2	3	6	6
1102111	Spirits	4	4	1.00	–	2	–	2	2	2	2	1	2	1	–	1	2	–	2	2	2	3	3	1
1102121	Wine	7	6	0.86	–	2	–	3	4	4	4	–	1	4	1	1	4	–	4	3	–	4	5	4
1102131	Beer	4	4	1.00	–	2	–	3	–	3	2	3	2	3	–	3	2	–	2	4	2	3	3	3
1102211	Tobacco	6	6	1.00	6	–	–	3	1	1	4	2	2	1	–	2	5	4	3	2	3	1	3	2
1102311	Narcotics	3	–	–	–	–	–	–	–	–	–	–	–	–	–	–	–	–	–	–	–	–	–	–
1103111	Clothing materials, other articles of clothing, and clothing accessories	8	3	0.38	3	1	1	3	–	2	3	1	1	2	1	1	1	2	1	2	2	1	1	3
1103121	Garments	66	22	0.33	16	9	15	16	14	16	16	15	6	12	9	10	15	5	11	17	19	19	16	19
1103141	Cleaning, repair, and hire of clothing	2	2	1.00	2	–	1	–	2	2	2	1	1	2	–	2	2	1	2	2	2	2	2	1
1103211	Shoes and other footwear	12	4	0.33	4	3	2	2	4	4	4	4	1	3	2	2	3	1	2	4	4	4	2	4
1103221	Repair and hire of footwear	2	2	1.00	2	1	1	2	2	2	–	–	1	2	–	1	2	2	1	2	–	2	2	2
1104311	Maintenance and repair of the dwelling	6	5	0.83	4	2	3	5	3	4	4	2	1	2	4	3	5	5	3	4	3	4	4	4
1104411	Water supply	1	1	1.00	1	1	1	1	1	1	–	1	–	1	1	1	–	–	–	1	–	1	1	1
1104421	Miscellaneous services relating to the dwelling	1	–	–	–	–	–	–	–	–	–	–	–	–	–	–	–	–	–	–	–	–	–	–
1104511	Electricity	2	1	0.50	1	–	2	1	1	1	1	1	–	–	–	1	–	1	–	1	1	1	1	1
1104521	Gas	2	2	1.00	2	1	–	1	–	2	1	–	–	1	1	1	1	2	–	2	1	1	1	1
1104531	Other fuels	3	3	1.00	2	–	–	3	–	1	2	1	1	2	1	–	1	3	1	2	2	–	1	2
1105111	Furniture and furnishings	18	5	0.28	4	3	–	4	3	3	3	1	2	2	1	1	4	2	3	4	3	3	2	5
1105121	Carpets and other floor coverings	3	3	1.00	2	2	1	3	2	2	–	1	1	1	1	1	1	2	–	1	–	1	1	2
1105131	Repair of furniture, furnishings, and floor coverings	2	–	–	–	–	–	–	–	–	–	–	–	–	–	–	–	–	–	–	–	–	–	–
1105211	Household textiles	10	3	0.30	2	1	2	3	2	2	1	1	3	2	1	2	1	1	1	2	1	3	2	2
1105311	Major household appliances whether electric or not	22	5	0.23	4	2	5	3	4	3	3	1	2	3	2	1	3	2	5	3	1	2	3	4
1105321	Small electric household appliances	27	6	0.22	4	4	3	4	4	5	3	1	2	4	4	3	3	2	3	5	3	5	4	3
1105331	Repair of household appliances	3	3	1.00	3	1	–	3	3	2	3	1	3	2	2	3	2	3	3	–	3	2	3	3
1105411	Glassware, tableware, and household utensils	14	5	0.36	5	2	4	2	2	4	5	3	–	2	3	2	5	3	3	5	2	5	4	4
1105521	Small tools and miscellaneous accessories	10	3	0.30	3	3	3	2	2	3	3	1	2	2	1	2	3	3	2	3	3	3	2	3
1105611	Nondurable household goods	12	3	0.25	1	2	2	1	1	1	3	1	2	2	2	2	3	1	3	2	2	2	1	2

continued on next page

Table 4.6 continued

Basic Heading Code	Basic Heading Description	Number of Items specified 2011	2016[b]	Ratio 2016 to 2011	Number of Household Consumption items Priced in 2016																				
					BAN	BHU	BRU	CAM	FIJ	HKG	IND	INO	LAO	MAL	MLD	MON	NEP	PAK	PHI	SIN	SRI	TAP	THA	VIE
(1)	(2)	(3)	(4)	(5)	(6)	(7)	(8)	(9)	(10)	(11)	(12)	(13)	(14)	(15)	(16)	(17)	(18)	(19)	(20)	(21)	(22)	(23)	(24)	(25)
1105621	Domestic services	2	2	1.00	1	1	1	1	1	2	1	1	–	1	–	1	1	1	1	2	1	2	1	–
1106111	Pharmaceutical products	109	11	0.10	2	1	3	–	1	4	4	2	–	4	2	1	3	1	4	1	2	2	6	2
1106121	Other medical products	14	4	0.29	1	1	3	3	2	4	1	2	1	3	2	2	3	2	2	2	2	3	3	3
1106131	Therapeutic appliances and equipment	11	3	0.27	3	–	3	3	1	3	2	–	–	2	2	2	2	3	3	3	3	3	2	2
1106211	Medical services	7	2	0.29	2	–	1	1	1	–	2	–	–	2	2	1	2	–	2	2	–	1	1	1
1106221	Dental services	4	4	1.00	4	–	–	4	3	4	2	3	1	1	–	–	2	2	3	4	2	4	2	1
1106231	Paramedical services	7	2	0.29	2	–	1	2	1	2	1	–	1	–	1	–	1	1	2	2	1	1	1	–
1107111	Motor cars[c]	5	2	0.40	2	1	8	–	1	4	1	–	1	1	–	3	1	1	12	9	1	6	1	–
1107121	Motor cycles[c]	10	2	0.20	2	–	1	–	–	1	1	–	1	1	–	2	1	–	3	1	1	–	1	–
1107131	Bicycles[c]	3	3	1.00	3	1	2	1	–	6	2	2	1	2	1	4	1	1	5	3	2	6	3	1
1107221	Fuels and lubricants for personal transport equipment	9	2	0.22	1	2	2	2	1	1	1	–	2	–	1	2	1	2	2	1	2	1	2	1
1107231	Maintenance and repair of personal transport equipment	12	4	0.33	4	2	2	3	3	2	4	4	2	4	1	4	3	3	4	2	3	4	4	3
1107311	Passenger transport by railway	6	2	0.33	1	–	–	–	–	2	1	–	–	1	–	1	–	1	1	1	–	2	–	–
1107321	Passenger transport by road	6	2	0.33	1	1	–	1	2	2	1	1	1	1	–	1	–	–	1	1	1	1	1	2
1107331	Passenger transport by air	6	2	0.33	2	1	1	–	1	1	–	2	1	1	1	1	1	2	1	–	–	2	–	2
1107341	Passenger transport by sea and inland waterway	5	2	0.40	–	–	–	–	1	1	–	–	–	–	1	–	1	–	1	–	–	1	–	–
1107361	Other purchased transport services	4	4	1.00	1	–	–	1	1	–	4	4	–	3	–	3	–	1	1	1	1	2	1	2
1108111	Postal services	2	2	1.00	–	1	–	2	1	1	–	–	1	–	2	1	–	2	2	1	1	1	1	1
1108211	Telephone and telefax equipment[c]	9	3	0.33	2	3	9	3	2	8	3	2	3	3	1	8	–	2	8	9	2	6	2	3
1108311	Telephone and telefax services	7	2	0.29	1	2	1	1	1	–	1	1	–	1	2	1	1	1	2	1	1	1	2	2
1109111	Audiovisual, photographic, and information-processing equipment[c]	29	6	0.21	5	7	18	5	6	23	4	4	3	2	1	21	1	3	26	21	8	13	2	5
1109141	Recording media	11	3	0.27	–	2	–	2	1	2	3	1	1	2	1	3	2	2	2	1	1	1	1	3
1109151	Repair of audiovisual, photographic, and information-processing equipment	2	2	1.00	1	1	–	2	1	–	1	–	–	1	1	–	1	–	1	–	–	–	1	1
1109211	Major durables for outdoor and indoor recreation	4	4	1.00	3	1	–	3	2	4	4	4	1	4	1	3	1	1	3	3	3	4	2	3
1109311	Other recreational items and equipment	12	4	0.33	3	2	1	2	1	4	2	1	1	1	3	2	1	2	4	4	2	4	3	2
1109331	Gardens and pets	5	2	0.40	2	–	–	2	–	1	–	–	–	1	1	2	1	1	2	2	–	2	1	1
1109351	Veterinary and other services for pets	1	1	1.00	–	–	–	–	1	1	1	1	–	–	–	–	–	–	1	1	1	–	1	–

continued on next page

Table 4.6 continued

Number of Household Consumption items Priced in 2016

Basic Heading Code	Basic Heading Description	Number of Items specified 2011	Number of Items specified 2016[b]	Ratio 2016 to 2011	BAN	BHU	BRU	CAM	FIJ	HKG	IND	INO	LAO	MAL	MLD	MON	NEP	PAK	PHI	SIN	SRI	TAP	THA	VIE
(1)	(2)	(3)	(4)	(5)	(6)	(7)	(8)	(9)	(10)	(11)	(12)	(13)	(14)	(15)	(16)	(17)	(18)	(19)	(20)	(21)	(22)	(23)	(24)	(25)
1109411	Recreational and sporting services	4	4	1.00	2	2	1	–	1	4	3	1	–	2	2	1	–	–	1	2	3	3	1	3
1109421	Cultural services	6	2	0.33	–	–	2	2	2	1	1	1	1	–	2	1	2	1	2	2	1	–	1	1
1109511	Newspapers, books, and stationery	9	3	0.33	2	1	1	3	2	2	3	1	2	2	2	1	2	2	1	2	2	2	3	1
1109611	Package holidays	7	2	0.29	2	–	–	–	–	2	–	–	1	2	1	1	–	–	–	2	–	2	2	1
1110111	Education	8	2	0.25	1	1	1	2	1	2	1	1	2	1	1	1	2	1	1	2	2	2	1	1
1111111	Catering services	17	5	0.29	4	2	2	4	1	3	5	1	–	3	–	3	2	3	2	5	2	2	1	4
1111211	Accommodation services	4	4	1.00	3	3	1	3	4	3	4	3	4	3	3	1	1	4	2	3	3	2	–	4
1112111	Hairdressing salons and personal grooming establishments	6	2	0.33	2	2	1	2	–	2	2	–	1	1	1	–	1	–	–	2	–	2	–	1
1112121	Appliances, articles, and products for personal care	18	5	0.28	4	4	5	5	4	5	4	1	3	2	5	2	5	4	4	5	3	5	5	3
1112311	Jewellery, clocks, and watches	10	3	0.30	3	1	2	3	2	1	2	–	1	3	3	1	3	3	1	3	3	1	2	3
1112321	Other personal effects	5	2	0.40	2	2	1	2	2	2	1	1	1	–	–	2	2	1	1	1	2	1	1	2
1112511	Insurance	6	2	0.33	–	1	–	1	2	2	1	1	1	1	1	1	2	1	2	1	–	2	–	1
1112621	Other financial services n.e.c.	6	2	0.33	1	1	–	1	2	2	2	1	2	2	1	1	2	1	2	1	–	2	1	1
1112711	Other services n.e.c.	2	1	0.50	1	–	–	1	1	1	1	1	1	1	1	1	–	1	–	–	1	1	1	1
	Total number of items priced	923	346	0.37	225	135	203	227	171	266	235	157	129	188	123	192	190	166	255	275	188	256	218	222
	Total number of basic headings priced for household consumption	96	93		82	68	68	82	81	88	85	72	73	84	68	83	81	77	85	88	77	88	86	84

– = magnitude equals zero; BAN = Bangladesh; BHU = Bhutan; BRU = Brunei Darussalam; CAM = Cambodia; FIJ = Fiji; HKG = Hong Kong, China; IND = India; INO = Indonesia; LAO = Lao People's Democratic Republic; MAL = Malaysia; MLD = Maldives; MON = Mongolia; n.e.c. = not elsewhere classified; NEP = Nepal; PAK = Pakistan; PHI = Philippines; SIN = Singapore; SRI = Sri Lanka; TAP = Taipei,China; THA = Thailand; VIE = Viet Nam.

Note: No items were priced for "Miscellaneous services relating to the dwelling" in 2016 and no core or fast-evolving products were identified for "Repair of furniture, furnishings, and floor coverings"; Total number of items priced by economies only includes those used for PPP calculations or prices after capital-to-national adjustment and exclusion of outliers.

[a] 2011 refers to the full list of items in the 2011 International Comparison Program and 2016 refers to the core list of items in the 2016 purchasing power parity research study.

[b] Only includes core items.

[c] The core items identified were supplemented by additional 44 fast-evolving items for the basic headings of: "Motorcars"–12 items; "Motorcycles"–2 items; "Bicycles"–3 items; "Telephone and telefax equipment"–7 items; "Audiovisual, photographic and information-processing equipment"–20 items that were priced in the 2016 list of household items, taking the total number of items in the list to 390.

Source: Asian Development Bank.

Dwelling services. No price survey on housing rentals was conducted in 2016 because, for comparability with 2011, the study team decided to use the reference volume approach, which was followed in the ICP's 2011 cycle.

Converting Capital-City Prices to National Average Prices for Household Products

Unlike nonhousehold product prices, which were collected only in capital cities for both the ICP's 2011 cycle and this research study, it was necessary to convert the household product average prices collected in 2016 from the capital-city level to the national average.

However, there was no need to make such price adjustments for items in the following cases:

(i)   No adjustments were made to item prices for Hong Kong, China; Singapore; and Taipei,China.
(ii) Prices for fast-evolving products were not adjusted.
(iii) Prices for durable goods were not adjusted.

Where adjustments were needed, two possible options for converting capital-city prices to national average prices were originally considered:

(i)   calculating adjustment factors using consumer price indexes (CPIs) where the CPI data allow it, i.e., intraeconomy adjustments to obtain national average price; or
(ii) calculating adjustment factors using the economies' price submissions during the ICP's 2011 cycle.

The first option was not implemented due to nonavailability of data and complexities in mapping the detailed CPI prices to ICP item prices. Hence, in practice, the second option was the relevant approach used. Capital-city-to-national (C→N)

adjustment factors were calculated as the ratios of average capital-city prices for each item to average national prices observed in the ICP's 2011 cycle. These adjustment factors for any item were defined under the condition that the item price was available for both 2011 and 2016. For any exceptions, the adjustment factor was taken as 1.

$$AF^{2011}_{C \to N} = \frac{\text{Average capital city price in 2011}}{\text{Average national price in 2011}}$$

These adjustment factors were used in estimating national average prices for each corresponding item priced in the core product list in 2016:

2016 National Average Prices =
$$\frac{\text{Observed capital city average prices in 2016}}{AF^{2011}_{C \to N}}$$

Validation of Price Data for the 2016 Update

The standard ICP practice of intraeconomy validation, followed by intereconomy validation based on Dikhanov tables, was implemented in the evaluation of the 2016 prices. Prices with overall CPD residuals greater than 0.25— for comparisons within basic headings or for comparisons of all items—were tagged for further examination and validation. Item prices with CPD residuals greater than 1.5 for all prices in the CPD regression, and item prices with CPD residuals greater than 0.75 for basic heading CPD regressions, were dropped as outliers.

Used as the denominator in the calculation of 2016 national average prices of the core list of household items, the *adjustment factor* came from the ICP's 2011 item price data. In the absence of an adjustment factor, the capital-city prices collected in an economy in 2016 but with no corresponding price available in 2011 were not included. The 2016 national prices calculated using adjustment factor $AF^{2011}_{C \to N}$ were then evaluated for consistency with the 2011 and 2017 national average prices. Prices evaluated as significantly implausible from the prices for their comparable items in 2011 or 2017 were excluded from further calculation of PPPs. The price data of household items available after this process were used in calculating the core-list PPPs for 2016.

Calculating Purchasing Power Parities for 2016

The calculation of the basic-heading level PPPs under all main aggregates was based on the CPD method, while PPPs for aggregates above the basic-heading level were calculated using the Gini-Éltető-Köves-Szulc (GEKS) method—both are recommended methods for ICP cycles (Chapter 3). As the 2016 price data for household items are based on the core product lists identified using the combinatorial approach, a few additional adjustments are necessary in estimating basic-heading level PPPs that can be used as inputs into the calculation of PPPs for higher-level aggregates.

Converting Purchasing Power Parities for Household Consumption from Core List to Full List

As this research study was based on the core-list approach for pricing household products, a two-stage process was followed in the compilation of PPPs at the basic-heading level for household consumption. At the first stage, the unadjusted basic heading PPPs for 2016 were calculated using the CPD method from the prices of the products in the core lists. This process recognizes that the basic heading PPPs based on the core list only provide an approximation of the basic heading PPPs derived when using prices for the full list of items in the basic heading. At the second stage, an adjustment factor was used to convert the 2016 basic heading PPPs derived from the core list to 2016 basic heading PPPs that would be derived using the full list of products.

Since prices were available for items in both the core and full lists in 2011, two sets of basic heading PPPs—one based on the core product list and the other on

the full product list—can be estimated. With these two sets of PPPs, it is possible to derive an adjustment factor for each basic heading, which can then be applied to the unadjusted basic-heading level PPPs for 2016, based on the core list in the first stage.

It must be noted that, for the purpose of this study, the ICP classification and methods used in the ICP's 2017 cycle were applied. Accordingly, the ICP's 2011 core-list and full-list PPPs were revised using the classification and methods followed for the ICP's 2017 cycle, and then recalculated for the same 20 economies that participated in this research study to derive the adjustment factors.

Let $\{PPP_{BH,j}^{2011,Core}$ and $PPP_{BH,j}^{2011,Full}: j = 1,2,\ldots,20\}$ represent, respectively, PPPs for a basic heading BH for economy j, calculated using the 2011 basic heading price data for the core list and full list of items used in the ICP's 2011 cycle. Then, the adjustment factor used for 2016 basic heading BH is defined as:

$$ADJ_{BH,j}^{2016} = \frac{PPP_{BH,j}^{2011,Core}}{PPP_{BH,j}^{2011,Full}} \text{ for } j = 1,2,\ldots,20$$

For example, if PPPs based on the core and full lists in 2011 for a basic heading are, respectively, 2.95 and 3.25 currency units per Hong Kong dollar, then the adjustment factor is 0.91 (obtained by dividing 2.95 by 3.25). The PPP for the full list under the same basic heading in 2016 is obtained by dividing the PPP for that basic heading (based on the core sample) by 0.91. Table 4.7 shows the adjustment factors for major aggregates calculated using data from the ICP's 2011 cycle.

Table 4.7 serves two purposes. First, it shows how the PPPs from the core list sample for household products deviate from the PPPs derived from the full household product list for different levels of aggregates. This deviation can be used in assessing the precision of the core sample approach. The table shows the precision (measured as the coefficient of variation of individual deviations) for each category of household basic headings, aggregated to a higher

Table 4.7: Coefficients of Variation and Adjustment Factors for Purchasing Power Parities from Core List to Full List for 2011 by Major Expenditure Category and by Economy[a]
(Asia and the Pacific=1.000)

Expenditure Category (1)	CV[b] (2)	BAN (3)	BHU (4)	BRU (5)	CAM (6)	FIJ (7)	HKG (8)	IND (9)	INO (10)	LAO (11)	MAL (12)	MLD (13)	MON (14)	NEP (15)	PAK (16)	PHI (17)	SIN (18)	SRI (19)	TAP (20)	THA (21)	VIE (22)
Gross Domestic Product	0.008	1.000	1.001	0.988	1.003	1.014	0.997	1.002	0.998	0.999	0.992	0.991	0.995	1.004	1.019	1.008	1.003	0.997	0.985	1.004	1.001
Actual individual consumption by households[c]	0.012	1.000	1.001	0.979	1.007	1.020	0.997	1.003	0.998	1.000	0.988	0.986	0.994	1.003	1.023	1.013	1.009	0.995	0.979	1.006	1.002
Food and nonalcoholic beverages	0.013	0.991	1.024	0.984	0.992	1.024	1.008	0.996	1.015	0.990	1.008	1.011	1.001	1.001	1.000	0.997	0.989	1.015	0.975	0.997	0.983
Food	0.014	0.992	1.028	0.984	0.991	1.026	1.008	0.997	1.015	0.987	1.008	1.010	1.002	0.999	0.998	0.993	0.989	1.017	0.973	0.999	0.983
Bread and cereals	0.043	0.947	1.094	0.979	1.030	1.043	1.020	0.986	0.982	0.942	0.976	1.029	0.945	0.984	1.016	1.055	1.009	0.929	0.985	1.039	1.024
Meat and fish	0.040	0.994	0.995	0.992	0.981	0.982	1.019	0.963	1.055	1.025	1.021	0.974	1.065	1.025	1.002	0.977	0.926	1.099	0.953	0.993	0.973
Fruits and vegetables	0.033	0.990	1.007	1.002	0.981	1.071	0.944	1.033	0.997	1.000	0.999	1.000	0.965	1.018	0.975	1.003	1.060	1.042	0.968	0.973	0.961
Other food and nonalcoholic beverages	0.026	1.051	1.002	0.973	1.003	1.018	1.021	0.998	1.019	0.986	1.019	1.033	0.973	1.002	1.007	0.958	0.996	1.037	1.003	0.993	0.963
Clothing and footwear	0.034	0.982	1.022	0.956	0.986	0.981	1.036	1.073	1.025	0.992	0.987	1.053	0.953	0.969	0.972	1.001	1.014	1.041	0.989	1.019	0.957
Clothing	0.042	0.975	1.027	0.953	0.969	0.974	1.012	1.115	1.026	0.984	0.988	1.045	0.960	0.961	0.974	0.995	1.024	1.060	0.995	1.027	0.952
Housing, water, electricity, gas, and other fuels[c]	0.011	0.993	1.015	0.983	1.012	1.012	1.003	1.006	0.987	0.999	0.992	0.991	0.987	1.000	1.000	1.023	1.007	1.004	0.985	1.002	0.999
Health and education[c]	0.079	1.093	0.987	0.947	0.946	0.996	0.932	1.060	0.992	0.987	1.016	0.900	0.934	1.120	1.236	0.981	0.971	0.952	0.934	1.050	1.020
Health[c]	0.053	1.015	0.962	0.964	0.955	0.994	0.987	0.977	1.019	1.035	1.005	0.951	1.025	1.017	1.139	0.970	1.065	0.935	0.926	0.990	1.096
Education[c]	0.131	1.155	1.004	0.923	0.938	0.994	0.881	1.157	0.942	0.942	1.016	0.874	0.872	1.222	1.381	0.980	0.905	0.966	0.951	1.095	0.949
Transportation and communication	0.068	0.982	0.949	0.994	1.085	1.112	1.056	0.925	0.973	1.057	0.918	0.984	1.071	0.884	0.942	1.117	1.051	0.950	0.971	0.959	1.063
Transportation	0.075	0.979	0.928	0.997	1.064	1.155	1.096	0.961	0.986	0.924	0.919	0.930	1.097	0.893	0.985	1.084	1.029	0.931	1.044	0.961	1.089
Recreation and culture[c]	0.035	0.971	0.963	0.972	1.041	1.029	1.018	0.955	0.989	0.963	1.030	0.927	1.036	1.038	1.038	1.027	0.998	1.022	1.026	1.003	0.967
Restaurants and hotels	0.044	0.990	1.076	0.975	1.039	0.929	0.990	1.023	0.996	0.964	1.013	1.067	0.928	1.073	1.029	0.940	1.027	0.973	1.003	1.008	0.976
Other consumption expenditure items[c]	0.010	0.998	0.990	0.991	1.012	1.006	0.995	1.005	0.992	1.009	0.993	1.001	0.983	1.003	0.993	0.988	1.018	1.007	0.993	1.011	1.013
Individual consumption expenditure by government	0.020	1.009	0.999	0.984	0.993	1.007	0.984	1.005	0.999	0.993	1.007	0.973	0.996	1.023	1.058	1.002	0.988	0.993	0.963	1.019	1.009
Collective consumption expenditure by government	0.005	1.000	1.001	0.988	1.003	1.006	0.999	1.002	0.999	1.001	0.994	0.996	0.996	1.002	1.011	1.004	1.006	0.999	0.993	1.002	1.000
Gross fixed capital formation	–	1.000	1.000	1.000	1.000	1.000	1.000	1.000	1.000	1.000	1.000	1.000	1.000	1.000	1.000	1.000	1.000	1.000	1.000	1.000	1.000
Machinery and equipment	–	1.000	1.000	1.000	1.000	1.000	1.000	1.000	1.000	1.000	1.000	1.000	1.000	1.000	1.000	1.000	1.000	1.000	1.000	1.000	1.000
Construction	–	1.000	1.000	1.000	1.000	1.000	1.000	1.000	1.000	1.000	1.000	1.000	1.000	1.000	1.000	1.000	1.000	1.000	1.000	1.000	1.000
Change in inventories and acquisitions less disposals of valuables	0.007	0.988	0.999	0.992	1.001	1.013	1.007	1.003	1.006	0.990	0.989	0.998	1.005	0.992	0.993	1.011	1.010	1.001	0.998	1.006	0.998
Balance of exports and imports	–	1.000	1.000	1.000	1.000	1.000	1.000	1.000	1.000	1.000	1.000	1.000	1.000	1.000	1.000	1.000	1.000	1.000	1.000	1.000	1.000
Individual consumption expenditure by households[d]	0.012	0.999	1.000	0.978	1.008	1.021	0.998	1.002	0.998	1.000	0.986	0.988	0.994	1.002	1.021	1.015	1.010	0.995	0.981	1.005	1.002
Government final consumption expenditure	0.010	1.003	1.000	0.986	0.998	1.007	0.992	1.003	0.999	0.999	0.999	0.990	0.997	1.010	1.027	1.003	1.002	0.996	0.978	1.010	1.003
Actual individual consumption by households[c]	0.012	1.000	1.001	0.979	1.007	1.020	0.997	1.003	0.998	1.000	0.988	0.986	0.994	1.003	1.023	1.013	1.009	0.995	0.979	1.006	1.002
All goods	0.016	0.979	0.989	0.983	0.995	1.013	1.021	0.999	1.021	0.984	0.985	0.980	1.014	0.981	0.997	1.022	1.028	0.992	0.998	1.012	1.009
Nondurables	0.015	0.998	1.000	0.969	0.999	1.022	1.020	1.009	1.009	0.993	0.970	1.004	1.006	0.998	1.008	1.013	0.989	1.004	0.978	0.995	1.018
Semidurables	0.032	0.985	1.016	0.984	0.965	0.983	1.029	1.051	1.055	1.013	0.972	1.042	0.943	1.009	0.966	0.991	1.021	1.010	0.997	1.024	0.952
Durables	0.099	0.914	0.892	1.018	1.006	0.995	1.035	0.869	1.056	0.936	1.097	0.842	1.145	0.904	0.955	1.181	1.143	0.912	1.063	1.104	1.026
Services	0.033	1.039	1.015	0.958	1.028	1.036	0.970	1.005	0.952	1.026	0.985	1.000	0.957	1.046	1.073	1.000	0.994	0.997	0.957	0.994	0.985

– = magnitude equals zero; BAN = Bangladesh; BHU = Bhutan; BRU = Brunei Darussalam; CAM = Cambodia; CV = coefficient of variation; FIJ = Fiji; HKG = Hong Kong, China; IND = India; INO = Indonesia; LAO = Lao People's Democratic Republic; MAL = Malaysia; MLD = Maldives; MON = Mongolia; NEP = Nepal; PAK = Pakistan; PHI = Philippines; SIN = Singapore; SRI = Sri Lanka; TAP = Taipei,China; THA = Thailand; VIE = Viet Nam

[a] The 2011 International Comparison Program data were used to estimate the ratios of the purchasing power parity (PPP) of the core and full lists by each major expenditure category. Purchasing power parity (PPP) ratios were derived for each basic heading and were used to adjust the final 2016 PPP core estimates to the full-list PPPs.

[b] Coefficients of variation of the adjustment factor.

[c] Includes individual consumption expenditure by households, nonprofit institutions serving households, and government.

[d] Includes expenditure by nonprofit institutions serving households.

Source: Asian Development Bank estimates.

level and by economy. It reveals that the overall precision for GDP is 0.8%, while that for individual consumption expenditure by households is 1.2%. Economies exhibiting high deviations for individual consumption expenditure by households include Brunei Darussalam (−2.2%); Fiji (+2.1%); Pakistan (+2.1%); and Taipei,China (−1.9%). Most other economies are within boundaries of 1.4%. These deviations quoted are for unadjusted PPPs. Once they are adjusted using the coefficients (adjustment factor) for each basic heading, the deviations become zero for all economies.

The second purpose of Table 4.7 is that its figures were used to adjust the PPPs based on the core product prices collected in 2016, with the objective of estimating the PPPs that would have been obtained if the whole product list were used for price collection.

Gap-Filling and Calibration

For the calculation of PPPs at levels of aggregation higher than the basic headings, it is necessary to have non-zero PPPs for all basic headings. During the implementation of the core item approach for the study on 2016 data, there were instances when some economies had no PPP data, since items in a specific basic heading were either not priced or had prices that were outliers. In these instances, gap-fill PPPs were imputed using the CPD method, by taking information from the calculated PPPs of related basic headings. A gap-fill matrix, composed of dummy or indicator variables that show which basic headings are relevant to the basic heading with missing PPPs, is used to fill in the gaps.

A second, similar problem was also encountered during this research study. Due to differences in the commodity baskets of each economy, items specific to a basic heading may not have been priced in 2016 in the reference economy, in this case Hong Kong, China. In such instances, the CPD method could not be implemented using Hong Kong, China as the reference economy. The CPD method was therefore implemented using an alternative economy as the reference economy. Gap-filling then imputed a PPP for Hong Kong, China, which would be different from 1. The PPPs for all the economies were then recalibrated to Hong Kong, China = 1.00 using the imputed PPP for Hong Kong, China. This ensured that the reference currency continued to be the Hong Kong dollar.

Purchasing Power Parities for Government Compensation

As the government compensation data were based on a complete list of government occupations, the basic-heading level PPPs were calculated using the CPD method and did not require any core-to-full adjustment process as with the household consumption basic heading PPPs. However, the PPPs needed to be adjusted to account for differentials in the productivity across economies. PPPs for government compensation were therefore adjusted using the Productivity Adjustment Factors introduced by Inklaar (2019). That is,

$$\text{Adjusted 2016 } PPP = \frac{2016 \; PPP}{\text{Inklaar's } PAF}$$

The adjusted government compensation PPPs were used for calculating higher-level aggregations. This minimized discrepancies between the productivity of employees across economies, since it was assumed that outputs produced using an hour of labor in an economy like Hong Kong, China would be different from the outputs produced using an hour of labor in another economy, Asia and the Pacific being a region with a diverse mix of government provisions (ADB 2020, 145-147).

Purchasing Power Parities for Construction

Construction data were based on a one-time survey for construction inputs. Unlike the 2009 update, which had only 10 inputs, this research study had 54 inputs for the calculation of PPPs for construction. Hence, no adjustments were made and the usual steps in an ICP benchmark year were followed.

Construction has three basic headings:

(i)   Civil engineering works
(ii) Residential buildings
(iii) Nonresidential buildings

Each of these has the following subheadings:

(i)   Materials
(ii) Equipment rental
(iii) Labor

PPPs for construction were estimated using the following steps:

(i)   One set of input prices were collected for materials, equipment rental, and labor. However, only relevant inputs were included in each of the three basic headings (civil engineering works, residential buildings, and nonresidential buildings) using product relevance information.

(ii) Unweighted PPPs for the subheadings (materials, equipment rental, and labor) under the three basic headings were calculated using the CPD method, resulting in nine sets of subheading PPPs. As with household consumption, there were some instances where subheading PPPs returned zero values, since some input items were not priced. These missing PPPs were filled using a relevant reference.

(iii) The subheading PPPs were aggregated using the GEKS method and resource mix as weights, resulting in 2016 PPPs for the three basic headings of construction—residential construction, nonresidential construction, and civil engineering—to be further used for higher-level aggregations.

Purchasing Power Parities for Machinery and Equipment

Machinery and equipment data were based on a one-time price survey of relevant items. In contrast to the 2009 update, which used a reduced list, this research study used a full range of representative products of machinery and equipment. This means that core-to-full adjustments were not needed. The PPPs at the basic-heading level were calculated using the CPD method.

Reference Purchasing Power Parities

Reference PPPs are used for some basic headings for which no price data are collected or, if collected, data were considered "bad" or noncomparable. Following the changes in ICP classification from 2011 to 2017, the 2017 ICP Reference PPP matrix was used in this study on 2016 data. This matrix identifies relevant basic headings that can be used to estimate the PPPs of the reference basic headings (Appendix 2).

Table 4.8 shows the number of basic headings that were priced and referenced in the ICP's 2017 cycle. In addition to these reference basic headings, and following the approach used in the ICP's 2011 cycle, it was decided to use the reference volume approach to estimate the PPPs for housing or dwelling services in the ICP's 2017 cycle. The same approach was used for this study on 2016 data.

National Accounts Expenditure Data

The national accounts data used in this research study were those from the gross domestic product expenditures series provided for the ICP's 2017 cycle. The process of revising and upgrading national accounts is ongoing in most economies, so significant revisions may occur in many economies' accounts. The estimates provided for the study may be revised in the coming years, so that the estimates of GDP and its major aggregates in this publication

Table 4.8: Number of Basic Headings by Category Used in the Study

Categories	Number of Basic Headings		
	Priced	Referenced	Total
Food and nonalcoholic beverages	29	–	29
Alcoholic beverages, tobacco, and narcotics	4	1	5
Clothing and footwear	5	–	5
Housing, water, electricity, gas, and other fuels	7	1	8
Furnishings, household equipment, and routine maintenance of the house	11	2	13
Health[a]	6	1	7
Transport	11	2	13
Communication	3	–	3
Recreation and culture	10	3	13
Education	1	–	1
Restaurants and hotels	2	–	2
Miscellaneous goods and services	4	7	11
Individual consumption expenditure by NPISHs	–	5	5
Individual consumption expenditure by government	2	19	21
Collective consumption expenditure by government	1	4	5
Gross capital formation	8	4	12
Balance of exports and imports	–	2	2
Total basic headings	104	51	155

– = magnitude equals zero; NPISHs = nonprofit institutions serving households.
Note: The basic headings used are the same as those used for the 2017 International Comparison Program.
[a] Number of products includes split items for pharmaceutical products.
Source: Asian Development Bank estimates.

aggregates had to be broken down by basic headings of ICP using best available sources of information. In addition to this, any statistical discrepancy reported in the 2016 GDP estimates was allocated by the economies to one or more basic headings as required in the ICP. Economies producing the GDP by fiscal year had to convert to 2016 calendar year. These processes may also lead to the individual expenditure aggregates not matching with the published estimates of expenditure aggregates.

Calculation of Purchasing Power Parities for Higher-Level Aggregates

After calculating PPPs for the 155 basic headings for all 20 participating economies, PPPs for each higher level of aggregation were calculated using the recommended GEKS as the index number method, with the component basic heading PPPs as inputs along with corresponding basic heading GDP expenditures, which serve as the weights in the aggregation process.

may differ from 2016 estimates contained in any individual economy's national accounts releases. More importantly, in deriving the required 155 basic heading weights for the study, some economies used their 2011 GDP structures when they were unable to produce their national accounts in time to meet the timetable. In some cases, they did not compile GDP expenditure-based estimates. In several cases, even when expenditure-based estimates of GDP were compiled, they did not have the required level of detail (155 basic headings). In such cases the higher

5. Overview of the Study Results

The research study on using a reduced information approach to update purchasing power parities (PPPs) for 2016 has yielded some interesting results. It is, however, important to first outline a few parameters used in achieving these results.

The expenditure side of gross domestic product (GDP) is the statistical basis for the intereconomy comparisons presented, with PPPs, price levels, and PPP-converted real expenditures calculated at the level of total GDP and for its main aggregates. It may be noted that, while the PPPs, real expenditures, and real expenditures per capita can be calculated for all 155 basic headings in the International Comparison Program (ICP) and at any desired level of aggregation up to and including total GDP, results at the detailed levels are generally less reliable than those at higher levels of aggregation. The results presented here are at higher aggregated levels, covering GDP and main aggregates for 20 participating economies.

All the results presented use Hong Kong, China as the reference economy and Hong Kong dollar as the numeraire currency, unless otherwise specified. The methodology used in the ICP ensures that price and real expenditure relativities remain the same, even when some other economy's currency is used as the numeraire currency. The PPPs express the values of local currencies in relation to a numeraire currency. If one economy's GDP is twice that of another economy when measured in Hong Kong dollars, its GDP would still be twice as large if it were measured in, say, Indian rupees. Only the absolute levels of GDP will change depending on the numeraire currency, but the relativities between the economies do not change.

The study results presented here relate to the following main aggregates: (i) gross domestic product;

(ii) individual consumption expenditure by households (ICEH); (iii) actual individual consumption by households (AICH); (iv) government final consumption expenditure (GFCE); and (v) gross fixed capital formation (GFCF). The presentation and discussion of results is structured around the following indicators: (i) PPPs and exchange rates; (ii) size and distribution of real expenditures for GDP and major expenditure aggregates; (iii) real expenditures per capita and relative rankings; and (iv) price levels.

Gross Domestic Product: Size and Distribution

GDP is a measure of economic activity as recommended for individual economies in the System of National Accounts 2008 (United Nations 2009). It is calculated as the gross value of output *minus* the value of goods and services used as intermediate outputs *plus* any taxes less subsidies not already included in the value of the output. This notion of GDP measures economic activity from the production side. From the expenditure side, an equivalent measure of GDP is the market value of all final goods and services produced within an economy in a given year. The ICP conceptual framework is set around the expenditure side of GDP because data on GDP expenditures, and the prices of the products underlying those expenditures, enable statisticians to analyze price and quantity (or volume) components of GDP. The expenditure measure of GDP also provides more direct indicators of the standards of living in participating economies. Comparable measures of real GDP per capita provide valuable information on the ability of the general population to access goods and services for their consumption.

Table 5.1 presents summary results at the GDP level for the 20 participating economies in 2016. Column 2 shows the estimated PPPs for GDP. For example, at the GDP level, the PPP for the Bangladesh taka against the Hong Kong dollar is HK$1.00 = Tk4.81. A comparison of PPPs in Column 2 with the corresponding exchange rates in Column 3 shows that the PPPs for all economies were lower than their exchange rates in 2016. In many cases, the PPPs were less than 50% of the exchange rates. In the case of Singapore, the PPP was closer to the exchange rate. An immediate implication is that real GDP expenditures, obtained by converting GDP in local currency units using PPPs, would be significantly higher than the nominal expenditures obtained using exchange rates as conversion factors. This also means that the distribution of real expenditures across economies would be more equal when compared to the distribution of nominal expenditures. It can be seen that the total size of the 20 economies of Asia and the Pacific, measured in real and nominal

terms, are HK$104.244 trillion and HK$48.477 trillion, respectively, implying that the real expenditure of all 20 economies at the GDP level is more than 2.1 times the nominal expenditures (with Hong Kong, China as the reference economy for real and nominal measures).

Figure 5.1 shows that, for all economies, nominal GDP (based on expenditures) was much lower than real GDP, with the exception of Hong Kong, China, which is the reference economy (where the two values were obviously equal). The largest economy in Asia and the Pacific, both in real and nominal terms, was India; the smallest was Bhutan. India's economy was approximately 1,000 times larger than that of Bhutan in both real and nominal terms, but this disparity is partly reflective of the relative population sizes of the two economies. India; Indonesia; Thailand; Taipei,China; and Pakistan were the five largest economies among the 20 that participated in the study.

Figure 5.1: Real and Nominal Gross Domestic Product, 2016
(HK$ billion)

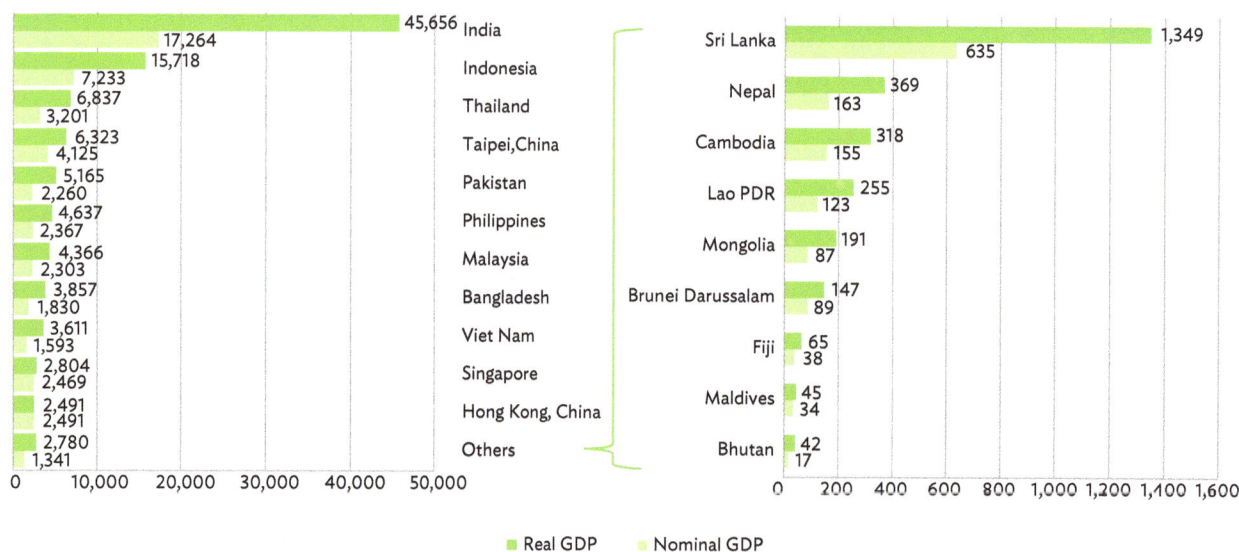

GDP = gross domestic product, HK$ = Hong Kong dollar, Lao PDR = Lao People's Democratic Republic.
Source: Asian Development Bank estimates.

Table 5.1: Summary Results for Gross Domestic Product, 2016
(Hong Kong, China as base)

Economy	PPPs (HK$ = 1.00)	Exchange Rates (HK$ = 1.00)	Expenditure (HK$ billion) Based on PPPs	Based on XRs	Expenditure per Capita (HK$) Based on PPPs	Based on XRs	Expenditure per Capita Indexes — Asia and the Pacific = 100 Based on PPPs	Based on XRs	HKG = 100 Based on PPPs	Based on XRs	Shares (Asia and the Pacific = 100.00) Expenditure Based on PPPs	Based on XRs	Population	PLIs Asia and the Pacific = 100	HKG=100	Reference Data Population (million)	Expenditure in LCU (billion)
(1)	(2)	(3)	(4)	(5)	(6)	(7)	(8)	(9)	(10)	(11)	(12)	(13)	(14)	(15)	(16)	(17)	(18)
Bangladesh	4.81	10.13	3,857	1,830	24,118	11,445	54	55	7	3	3.70	3.78	6.89	102	47	159.90	18,543
Bhutan	3.55	8.66	42	17	57,791	23,712	129	114	17	7	0.04	0.04	0.03	88	41	0.73	149
Brunei Darussalam	0.11	0.18	147	89	348,474	209,926	776	1,005	103	62	0.14	0.18	0.02	130	60	0.42	16
Cambodia	255.51	522.88	318	155	20,851	10,189	46	49	6	3	0.31	0.32	0.66	105	49	15.25	81,242
Fiji	0.16	0.27	65	38	74,336	43,985	166	211	22	13	0.06	0.08	0.04	127	59	0.87	10
Hong Kong, China	1.00	1.00	2,491	2,491	339,478	339,478	756	1,626	100	100	2.39	5.14	0.32	215	100	7.34	2,491
India	3.27	8.66	45,656	17,264	35,147	13,291	78	64	10	4	43.80	35.61	55.95	81	38	1,299.00	149,452
Indonesia	789.01	1,714.49	15,718	7,233	60,757	27,960	135	134	18	8	15.08	14.92	11.14	99	46	258.71	12,401,729
Lao People's Democratic Republic	506.58	1,053.72	255	123	37,601	18,077	84	87	11	5	0.24	0.25	0.29	103	48	6.79	129,279
Malaysia	0.28	0.53	4,366	2,303	137,901	72,755	307	348	41	21	4.19	4.75	1.36	113	53	31.66	1,231
Maldives	1.52	1.98	45	34	94,739	72,701	211	348	28	21	0.04	0.07	0.02	165	77	0.47	68
Mongolia	125.44	275.73	191	87	61,793	28,112	138	135	18	8	0.18	0.18	0.13	98	45	3.09	23,943
Nepal	6.11	13.83	369	163	12,983	5,737	29	27	4	2	0.35	0.34	1.22	95	44	28.39	2,253
Pakistan	5.91	13.50	5,165	2,260	26,431	11,564	59	55	8	3	4.95	4.66	8.42	94	44	195.40	30,499
Philippines	3.12	6.12	4,637	2,367	44,917	22,924	100	110	13	7	4.45	4.88	4.45	110	51	103.24	14,480
Singapore	0.16	0.18	2,804	2,469	500,134	440,315	1,114	2,109	147	130	2.69	5.09	0.24	189	88	5.61	439
Sri Lanka	8.83	18.76	1,349	635	63,618	29,942	142	143	19	9	1.29	1.31	0.91	101	47	21.20	11,907
Taipei,China	2.72	4.16	6,323	4,125	268,818	175,363	599	840	79	52	6.07	8.51	1.01	140	65	23.52	17,176
Thailand	2.13	4.55	6,837	3,201	101,354	47,451	226	227	30	14	6.56	6.60	2.91	101	47	67.46	14,555
Viet Nam	1,247.01	2,825.86	3,611	1,593	38,955	17,190	87	82	11	5	3.46	3.29	3.99	95	44	92.69	4,502,733
Asia and the Pacific	n.a.	n.a.	104,244	48,477	44,899	20,880	100	100	13	6	100.00	100.00	100.00	100	n.a.	2,321.72	n.a.

HK$ = Hong Kong dollar; HKG = Hong Kong, China; LCU = local currency unit; n.a. = not applicable; PLI = price level index; PPP = purchasing power parity; XR = exchange rate.
Sources: Asian Development Bank estimates (expenditures in local currency units and midyear population estimates were supplied by the economies that participated in the research study). For exchange rates: International Monetary Fund. International Financial Statistics. http://data.imf.org/ (accessed 17 September 2019).

Figure 5.2 shows the share of each economy in terms of real and nominal GDP as a proportion of the totals for all 20 participating economies. The five largest economies accounted for more than 75% of the total real GDP, whereas the five smallest economies (Bhutan, Maldives, Fiji, Brunei Darussalam, and Mongolia) accounted for less than 0.5% of the total real GDP.

Real and Nominal Income Per Capita

Per capita measures of income adjust for relative sizes of population and provide an indication of relative standards of living. Real GDP per capita (also described as real income per capita) is a measure commonly used for comparing standards of living across economies.

Figure 5.3 outlines real and nominal GDP per capita in each of the 20 economies that participated in this study (also found in Columns 6 and 7 of Table 5.1). It shows that the five richest economies in terms of real income per capita were Singapore; Brunei Darussalam; Hong Kong, China; Taipei,China; and Malaysia. The rankings of Hong Kong, China and Brunei Darussalam were reversed when nominal income per capita was considered. While India was the largest

economy by size of real GDP but ranked 16th among 20 economies in terms of real GDP per capita. Nepal was the economy with the lowest GDP per capita in both real and nominal terms.

Figure 5.4 shows an index of real GDP per capita for each economy, expressed relative to the Asia and Pacific region, and with the region's index set to 100. For Singapore, real income per capita in 2016 was roughly 11 times the size of the regional average, whereas for Nepal it was less than one-third of the average. For seven economies of the region, real GDP per capita was below the regional average.

Relative disparities in standards of living can be examined using the Lorenz curve for real and nominal income per capita. The Lorenz curve in Figure 5.5 plots the cumulative percentage shares of real expenditure against the cumulative percentage shares of population of the 20 economies, starting from the economy with the lowest real GDP per capita and progressing to the economy with the highest. The 45-degree line represents the line of equality; the areas between the line of equality and the curve lines representing per capita distribution represent inequality. From the

Figure 5.2: Economy Shares of Real and Nominal Gross Domestic Product, 2016
(%)

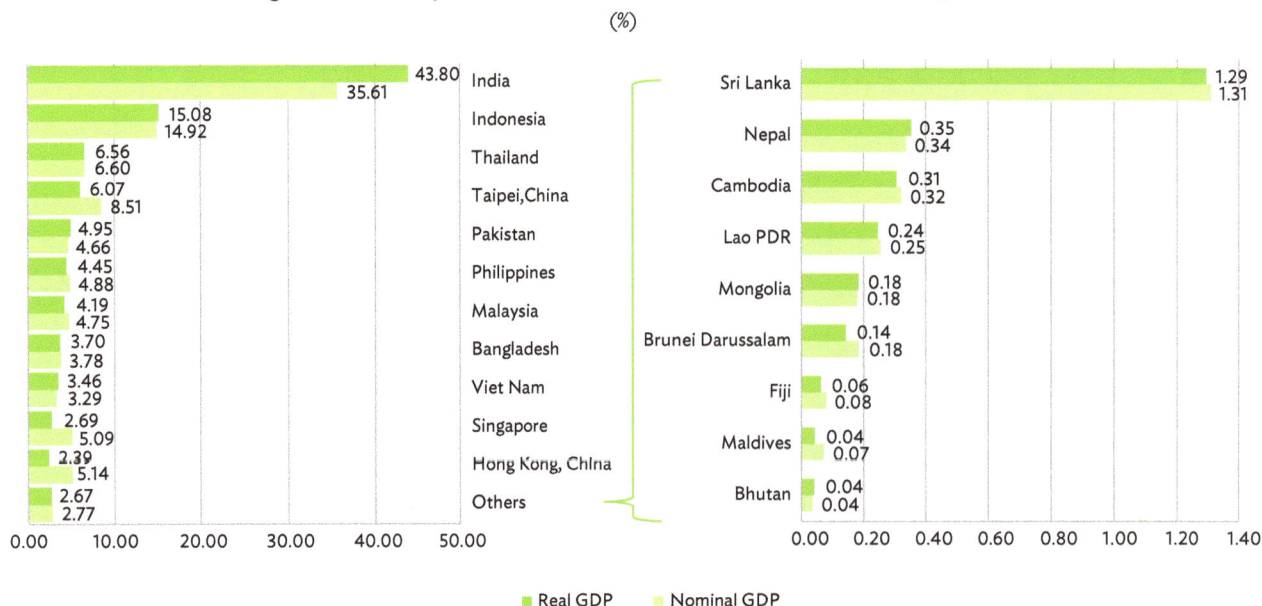

GDP = gross domestic product, Lao PDR = Lao People's Democratic Republic.
Source: Asian Development Bank estimates.

Figure 5.3: Real and Nominal Gross Domestic Product Per Capita, 2016

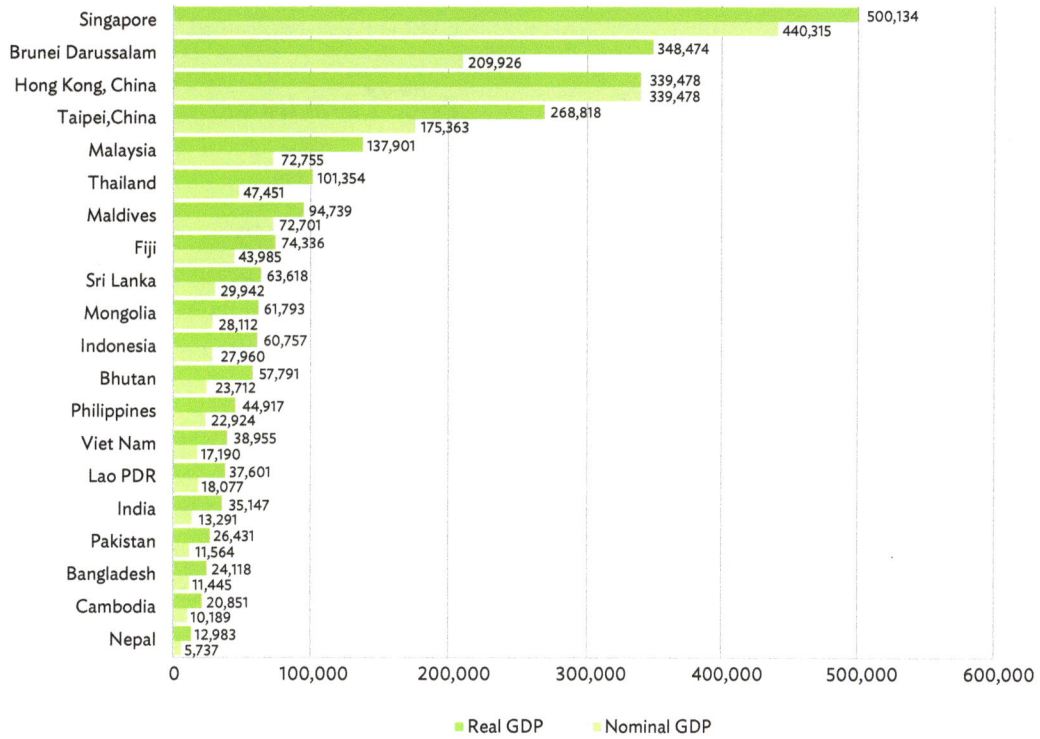

(HK$)

Country	Real GDP	Nominal GDP
Singapore	440,315	500,134
Brunei Darussalam	209,926	348,474
Hong Kong, China	339,478	339,478
Taipei,China	268,818	175,363
Malaysia	137,901	72,755
Thailand	101,354	47,451
Maldives	94,739	72,701
Fiji	74,336	43,985
Sri Lanka	63,618	29,942
Mongolia	61,793	28,112
Indonesia	60,757	27,960
Bhutan	57,791	23,712
Philippines	44,917	22,924
Viet Nam	38,955	17,190
Lao PDR	37,601	18,077
India	35,147	13,291
Pakistan	26,431	11,564
Bangladesh	24,118	11,445
Cambodia	20,851	10,189
Nepal	12,983	5,737

■ Real GDP   ■ Nominal GDP

GDP = gross domestic product, HK$ = Hong Kong dollar, Lao PDR = Lao People's Democratic Republic.
Source: Asian Development Bank estimates.

Figure 5.4: Index of Real Gross Domestic Product Per Capita, 2016

(Asia and the Pacific = 100)

Country	Index
Singapore	1,114
Brunei Darussalam	776
Hong Kong, China	756
Taipei,China	599
Malaysia	307
Thailand	226
Maldives	211
Fiji	166
Sri Lanka	142
Mongolia	138
Indonesia	135
Bhutan	129
Philippines	100
Viet Nam	87
Lao PDR	84
India	78
Pakistan	59
Bangladesh	54
Cambodia	46
Nepal	29

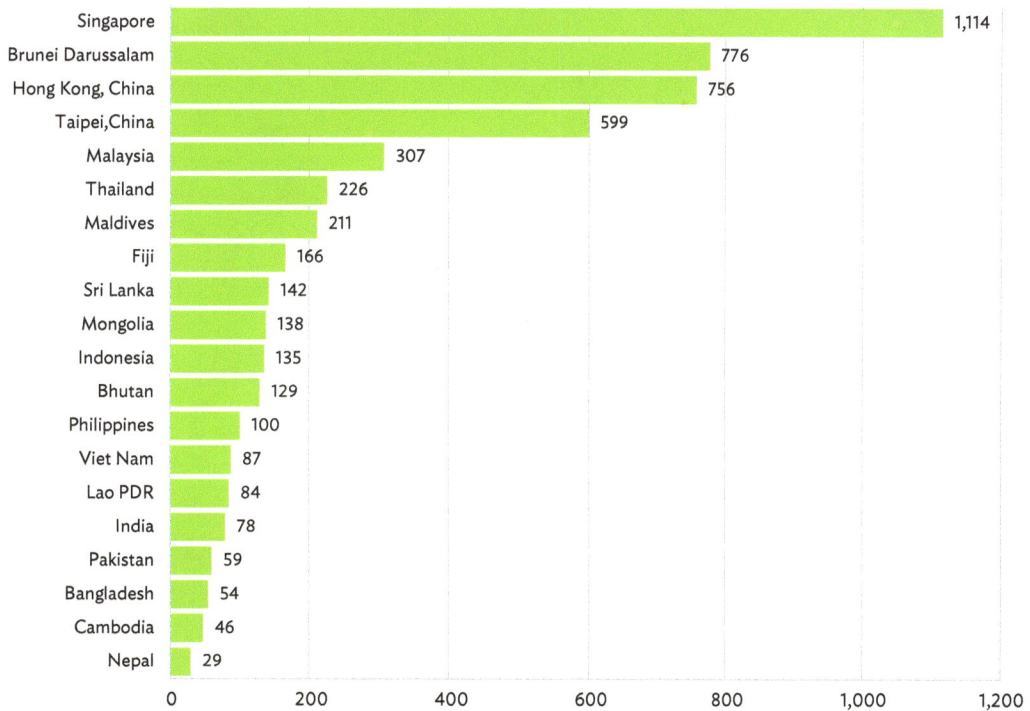

Lao PDR = Lao People's Democratic Republic.
Source: Asian Development Bank estimates.

Figure 5.5: Lorenz Curves for Real and Nominal Gross Domestic Product Per Capita, 2016

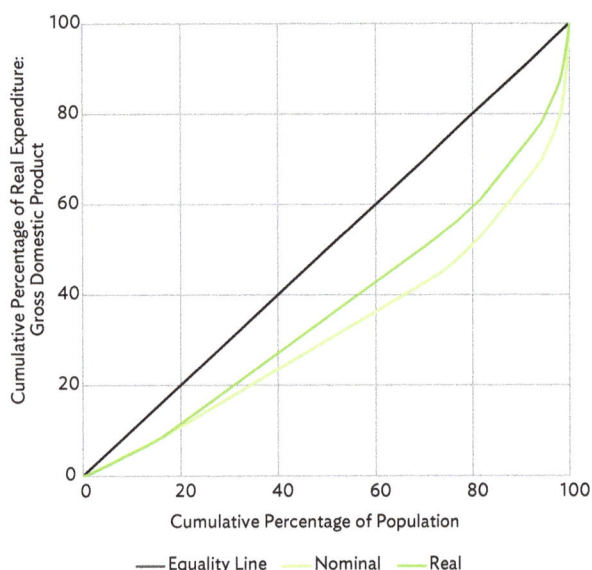

Note: Expenditure is represented by the economy-specific gross domestic product per capita.
Source: Asian Development Bank estimates.

figure, it can be seen that, across the 20 economies, the distribution of GDP per capita is more equal when real GDP is used, compared to using nominal GDP.

Price Level Index

The price level index (PLI), defined as the ratio of the PPP to the exchange rate, is a measure of the general price level in an economy, expressed relative to Hong Kong, China and to the regional index of 100. These PLIs are shown in Columns 15 and 16 of Table 5.1. It is clear from these columns that, for 2016, the price levels in all economies were lower than the level in Hong Kong, China.

Figure 5.6 plots the PLIs (Asia and the Pacific = 100) of the 20 participating economies against their real GDP per capita (in logarithmic scale). The figure shows that price levels in a majority of the economies were higher than the regional average of 100, as represented by the horizontal red line, in 2016. Further, there is a clear and positive association between the PLIs and real GDP per capita,

Figure 5.6: Price Level Index versus Real Gross Domestic Product Per Capita, 2016

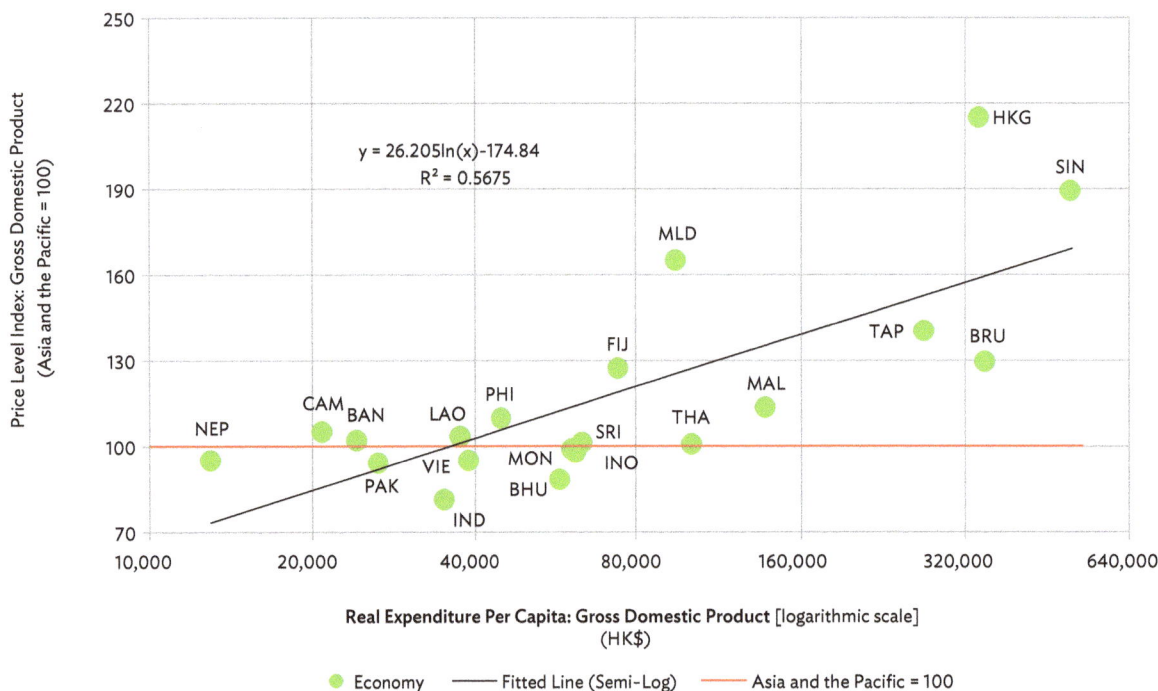

$y = 26.205\ln(x) - 174.84$
$R^2 = 0.5675$

BAN = Bangladesh; BHU = Bhutan; BRU = Brunei Darussalam; CAM = Cambodia; FIJ = Fiji; HK$ = Hong Kong dollar; HKG = Hong Kong, China; IND = India; INO = Indonesia; LAO = Lao People's Democratic Republic; MAL = Malaysia; MLD = Maldives; MON = Mongolia; NEP = Nepal; PAK = Pakistan; PHI = Philippines; SIN = Singapore; SRI = Sri Lanka; TAP = Taipei,China; THA = Thailand; VIE = Viet Nam.
Source: Asian Development Bank estimates.

Individual Consumption Expenditure by Households

A reliable indicator of material well-being in any given economy is household consumption expenditure or household final consumption. This aggregate as presented in this report combines individual consumption expenditure by households with expenditure by nonprofit institutions serving households (NPISHs). The main reason for considering these two together is that, in many economies, national accounts are not detailed enough to provide independent estimates of expenditures by NPISHs. These estimates can be obtained from household expenditure surveys, where households are asked to report the part of consumption expenditure that is provided by NPISHs. Results from the ICP for individual consumption expenditure by households (ICEH) are also of critical importance when it comes to poverty assessment in the Asia and Pacific region as well as in the world. The original international poverty line of $1 per day—a measure of extreme poverty—was based on PPPs for household consumption expenditure. Following the completion of the ICP's 2011 cycle, the international poverty line was set at $1.90 per day and is currently used for monitoring global and regional progress on the elimination of extreme poverty under the Sustainable Development Goals.

The total household expenditures by individuals and NPISHs are shown in real and nominal terms in Columns 4 and 5 of Table 5.2. For the 20 participating economies, these expenditures were HK$65.273 trillion and HK$28.615 trillion, respectively, in 2016. Real expenditure was roughly 2.3 times that of nominal expenditure, in large part due to the fact that the PPPs for ICEH were lower than the exchange rates, except in the case of Singapore with a PPP roughly the same as its exchange rate. The economy with the largest real ICEH was India, with HK$30.266 trillion,

which was roughly 1,780 times the economy with the smallest real ICEH, Maldives (HK$17 billion). India was then followed by Indonesia (HK$8.743 trillion), Pakistan (HK$4.366 trillion), and the Philippines (HK$3.648 trillion) as the next three economies with the largest real ICEH.

Adjusting for differences in population sizes (Figure 5.7) provides a different picture of the standard of consumption and the material well-being experienced by people living in different economies. Hong Kong, China had the highest ICEH per capita in 2016—about 31% higher than that of the second-ranked economy, Singapore. Singapore had the highest GDP per capita, but a much lower ICEH per capita (due to the substantial size of net exports in Singapore's GDP). While India was the largest economy in terms of total size of real ICEH, it was ranked 15th in terms of real ICEH per capita among the 20 economies. Nepal had the lowest real GDP per capita, below Cambodia and Bangladesh—the three lowest-ranked economies.

Actual Individual Consumption by Households

A comprehensive measure of goods and services consumed by households is actual individual consumption by households (AICH). This measure captures individual consumption expenditure by households and NPISHs *plus* expenditures by government on, predominantly, education and health services provided to households. These expenditures are termed "individual consumption expenditure" by the government because they are undertaken on behalf of households and are therefore part of a household's material well-being. Meanwhile, government services such as police, firefighting, and defense are classified as collective consumption expenditure because they are provided to the population as a whole. AICH is a better measure of material well-being than is overall GDP because it includes consumption by households from all three sources—consumption expenditure incurred by households, expenditure incurred by NPISHs on behalf of households, and government expenditure on behalf of households.

Table 5.2: Summary Results for Individual Consumption Expenditure by Households, 2016
(Hong Kong, China as base)

Economy	PPPs (HK$ = 1.00)	Exchange Rates (HK$ = 1.00)	Expenditure (HK$ billion) Based on PPPs	Based on XRs	Expenditure per Capita (HK$) Based on PPPs	Based on XRs	Expenditure per Capita Indexes — Asia and the Pacific = 100 Based on PPPs	Based on XRs	HKG = 100 Based on PPPs	Based on XRs	Shares (Asia and the Pacific = 100.00) — Expenditure Based on PPPs	Based on XRs	Population	PLIs — Asia and the Pacific = 100	HKG=100	Reference Data — Population (million)	Expenditure in LCU (billion)
(1)	(2)	(3)	(4)	(5)	(6)	(7)	(8)	(9)	(10)	(11)	(12)	(13)	(14)	(15)	(16)	(17)	(18)
Bangladesh	4.81	10.13	2,656	1,261	16,613	7,884	59	64	7	4	4.07	4.41	6.89	108	47	159.90	12,774
Bhutan	3.82	8.66	20	9	27,224	12,000	97	97	12	5	0.03	0.03	0.03	101	44	0.73	75
Brunei Darussalam	0.11	0.18	30	19	71,222	43,986	253	357	32	20	0.05	0.06	0.02	141	62	0.42	3
Cambodia	258.29	522.88	250	123	16,375	8,089	58	66	7	4	0.38	0.43	0.66	113	49	15.25	64,495
Fiji	0.15	0.27	45	25	51,232	29,300	182	238	23	13	0.07	0.09	0.04	130	57	0.87	7
Hong Kong, China	1.00	1.00	1,650	1,650	224,892	224,892	800	1,825	100	100	2.53	5.77	0.32	228	100	7.34	1,650
India	2.94	8.66	30,266	10,278	23,299	7,912	83	64	10	4	46.37	35.92	55.95	77	34	1,299.00	88,971
Indonesia	820.30	1,714.49	8,743	4,183	33,794	16,169	120	131	15	7	13.39	14.62	11.14	109	48	258.71	7,171,523
Lao People's Democratic Republic	547.75	1,053.72	128	66	18,791	9,768	67	79	8	4	0.20	0.23	0.29	119	52	6.79	69,857
Malaysia	0.28	0.53	2,370	1,263	74,868	39,891	266	324	33	18	3.63	4.41	1.36	122	53	31.66	675
Maldives	1.58	1.98	17	14	36,464	29,016	130	235	16	13	0.03	0.05	0.02	182	80	0.47	27
Mongolia	127.16	275.73	103	48	33,430	15,417	119	125	15	7	0.16	0.17	0.13	105	46	3.09	13,131
Nepal	6.12	13.83	311	138	10,971	4,855	39	39	5	2	0.48	0.48	1.22	101	44	28.39	1,907
Pakistan	5.66	13.50	4,366	1,831	22,343	9,368	79	76	10	4	6.69	6.40	8.42	96	42	195.40	24,708
Philippines	2.93	6.12	3,648	1,744	35,338	16,896	126	137	16	8	5.59	6.10	4.45	109	48	103.24	10,673
Singapore	0.18	0.18	875	898	156,134	160,174	555	1,300	69	71	1.34	3.14	0.24	234	103	5.61	160
Sri Lanka	9.24	18.76	822	405	38,782	19,111	138	155	17	8	1.26	1.42	0.91	112	49	21.20	7,600
Taipei,China	2.60	4.16	3,479	2,169	147,935	92,238	526	748	66	41	5.33	7.58	1.01	142	62	23.52	9,034
Thailand	2.12	4.55	3,328	1,550	49,344	22,979	176	186	22	10	5.10	5.42	2.91	106	47	67.46	7,048
Viet Nam	1,229.38	2,825.86	2,164	942	23,349	10,158	83	82	10	5	3.32	3.29	3.99	99	44	92.69	2,660,662
Asia and the Pacific	n.a.	n.a.	65,273	28,615	28,114	12,325	100	100	13	5	100.00	100.00	100.00	100	n.a.	2,321.72	n.a.

HK$ = Hong Kong dollar; HKG = Hong Kong, China; LCU = local currency unit; n.a. = not applicable; PLI = price level index; PPP = purchasing power parity; XR = exchange rate.
Note: In this table, incividual consumption expenditure by households includes expenditure by nonprofit institutions serving households.
Sources: Asian Development Bank estimates (expenditures in local currency units and midyear population estimates were supplied by the economies that participated in the research study). For exchange rates: International Monetary Fund. International Financial Statistics. http://data.imf.org/ (accessed 17 September 2019).

Figure 5.7: Real and Nominal Individual Consumption Expenditure by Households Per Capita, 2016
(HK$)

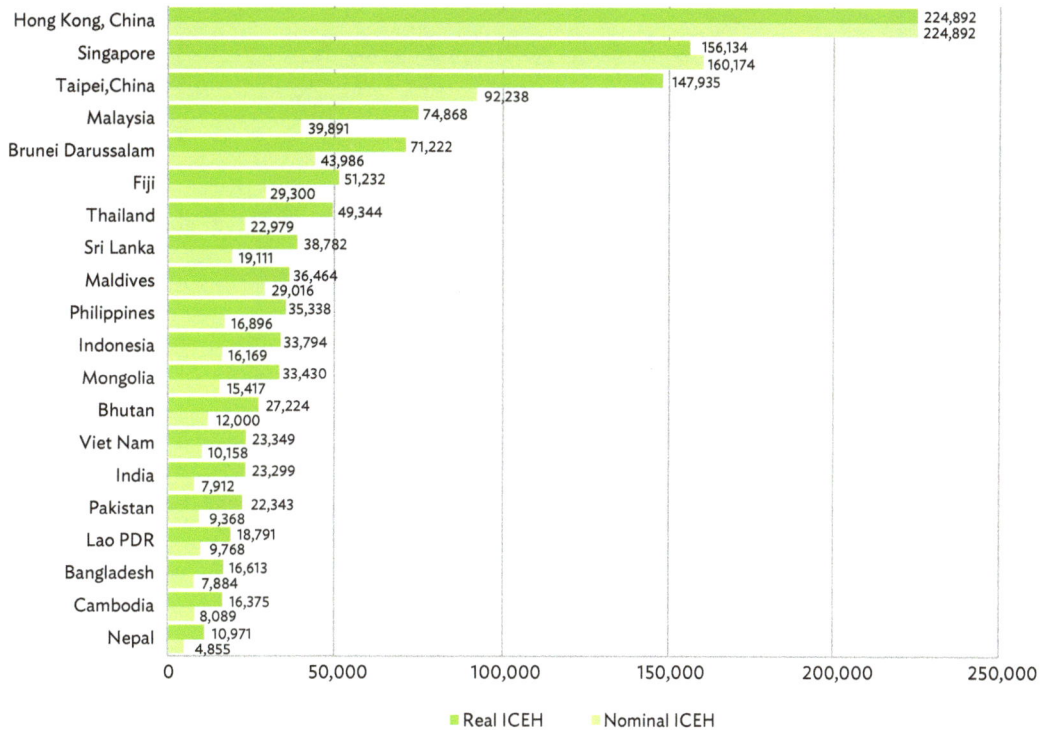

Economy	Real ICEH	Nominal ICEH
Hong Kong, China	224,892	224,892
Singapore	156,134	160,174
Taipei,China	147,935	92,238
Malaysia	74,868	39,891
Brunei Darussalam	71,222	43,986
Fiji	51,232	29,300
Thailand	49,344	22,979
Sri Lanka	38,782	19,111
Maldives	36,464	29,016
Philippines	35,338	16,896
Indonesia	33,794	16,169
Mongolia	33,430	15,417
Bhutan	27,224	12,000
Viet Nam	23,349	10,158
India	23,299	7,912
Pakistan	22,343	9,368
Lao PDR	18,791	9,768
Bangladesh	16,613	7,884
Cambodia	16,375	8,089
Nepal	10,971	4,855

■ Real ICEH   ■ Nominal ICEH

HK$ = Hong Kong dollar, ICEH = individual consumption expenditure by households, Lao PDR = Lao People's Democratic Republic.
Note: In this figure, individual consumption expenditure by households includes expenditure by nonprofit institutions serving households.
Source: Asian Development Bank estimates.

Table 5.3 shows comparisons of price levels and real expenditures for AICH in 2016. The total size of real AICH for the 20 participating economies was HK$70.975 trillion, compared to nominal AICH of HK$30.701 trillion. India had the largest total AICH both in real and nominal terms, with HK$31.755 trillion and HK$10.816 trillion, respectively. By contrast, the economy with the smallest real AICH was Maldives, with HK$21 billion. Columns 2 and 3 of Table 5.3 show that the PPPs for almost all economies were less than their exchange rates, meaning that their price levels for AICH (with Hong Kong, China as 100) would all be less than 100 (as shown in Column 16): India had the lowest PLI of 34. With reference to the regional average equal to 100, six of the 20 participating economies had PLIs less than 100. It should be noted that, as India had the largest share of real AICH expenditure (44.74%), the regional average price level is influenced by the price level for India.

Real AICH per capita is an appropriate indicator of welfare and material well-being. In 2016, Hong Kong, China had the highest real AICH per capita (HK$238,180), with Nepal recording the lowest (HK$11,783). Hong Kong, China posted real AICH per capita that was 7.79 times the regional average, 9.74 times the real AICH per capita of India, and 1.37 times that of Singapore.

Government Final Consumption Expenditure

Government final consumption expenditure (GFCE) is the sum of individual consumption expenditure by government (ICEG) and collective consumption expenditure by government (CCEG). ICEG is predominantly expenditure on health and education services provided to households, whereas CCEG

Table 5.3: Summary Results for Actual Individual Consumption by Households, 2016
(Hong Kong, China as base)

Economy	PPPs (HK$ =1.00)	Exchange Rates (HK$ =1.00)	Expenditure (HK$ billion)		Expenditure per Capita (HK$)		Expenditure per Capita Indexes				Shares (Asia and the Pacific = 100.00)			PLIs		Reference Data	
							Asia and the Pacific = 100		HKG = 100		Expenditure						
			Based on PPPs	Based on XRs	Based on PPPs	Based on XRs	Based on PPPs	Based on XRs	Based on PPPs	Based on XRs	Based on PPPs	Based on XRs	Population	Asia and the Pacific = 100	HKG=100	Population (million)	Expenditure in LCU (billion)
(1)	(2)	(3)	(4)	(5)	(6)	(7)	(8)	(9)	(10)	(11)	(12)	(13)	(14)	(15)	(16)	(17)	(18)
Bangladesh	4.62	10.13	2,828	1,288	17,689	8,057	58	61	7	3	3.99	4.20	6.89	105	46	159.90	13,054
Bhutan	3.55	8.66	23	10	32,124	13,158	105	100	13	6	0.03	0.03	0.03	95	41	0.73	83
Brunei Darussalam	0.11	0.18	41	25	97,114	58,601	318	443	41	25	0.06	0.08	0.02	139	60	0.42	4
Cambodia	245.83	522.88	278	131	18,224	8,568	60	65	8	4	0.39	0.43	0.66	109	47	15.25	68,317
Fiji	0.15	0.27	50	28	57,689	32,296	189	244	24	14	0.07	0.09	0.04	129	56	0.87	8
Hong Kong, China	1.00	1.00	1,747	1,747	238,180	238,180	779	1,801	100	100	2.46	5.69	0.32	231	100	7.34	1,747
India	2.95	8.66	31,755	10,816	24,446	8,327	80	63	10	3	44.74	35.23	55.95	79	34	1,299.00	93,634
Indonesia	782.41	1,714.49	9,741	4,445	37,654	17,184	123	130	16	7	13.73	14.48	11.14	106	46	258.71	7,621,743
Lao People's Democratic Republic	506.43	1,053.72	145	70	21,313	10,243	70	77	9	4	0.20	0.23	0.29	111	48	6.79	73,255
Malaysia	0.28	0.53	2,691	1,407	84,992	44,439	278	336	36	19	3.79	4.58	1.36	121	52	31.66	752
Maldives	1.52	1.98	21	16	43,919	33,820	144	256	18	14	0.03	0.05	0.02	178	77	0.47	32
Mongolia	114.77	275.73	127	53	41,119	17,116	135	129	17	7	0.18	0.17	0.13	96	42	3.09	14,577
Nepal	5.90	13.83	335	143	11,783	5,026	39	38	5	2	0.47	0.46	1.22	99	43	28.39	1,974
Pakistan	5.48	13.50	4,740	1,924	24,259	9,845	79	74	10	4	6.68	6.27	8.42	94	41	195.40	25,965
Philippines	2.90	6.12	3,950	1,869	38,258	18,105	125	137	16	8	5.57	6.09	4.45	109	47	103.24	11,437
Singapore	0.18	0.18	974	989	173,733	176,321	568	1,333	73	74	1.37	3.22	0.24	235	101	5.61	176
Sri Lanka	8.35	18.76	971	432	45,796	20,392	150	154	19	9	1.37	1.41	0.91	103	45	21.20	8,109
Taipei,China	2.57	4.16	4,022	2,478	170,992	105,337	559	797	72	44	5.67	8.07	1.01	142	62	23.52	10,317
Thailand	2.04	4.55	4,038	1,809	59,867	26,824	196	203	25	11	5.69	5.89	2.91	104	45	67.46	8,228
Viet Nam	1,155.82	2,825.86	2,497	1,021	26,934	11,016	88	83	11	5	3.52	3.33	3.99	95	41	92.69	2,885,540
Asia and the Pacific	n.a.	n.a.	70,975	30,701	30,570	13,223	100	100	13	6	100.00	100.00	100.00	100	n.a.	2,321.72	n.a.

HK$ = Hong Kong dollar; HKG = Hong Kong, China; LCU = local currency unit; n.a. = not applicable; PLI = price level index; PPP = purchasing power parity; XR = exchange rate.
Note: Actual individual consumption by households includes individual consumption expenditure by households and expenditure incurred by nonprofit institutions serving households and government on behalf of households.
Sources: Asian Development Bank estimates (expenditures in local currency units and midyear population estimates were supplied by the economies that participated in the research study). For exchange rates: International Monetary Fund. International Financial Statistics. http://data.imf.org/ (accessed 17 September 2019).

refers to services provided to the general population, including general administration, defense, police, firefighting, and environmental protection. Thus, ICEG is the part of government expenditure that has a direct bearing on the standard of living of the population, and its role is partly examined through the levels for AICH (because ICEG is one of the components of AICH). Comparative analyses of real GFCE per capita and its components provide useful insights into how governments play different roles in different economies.

The size of GFCE for the 20 participating economies in real terms was HK$12.646 trillion in 2016, compared to HK$5.329 trillion in nominal terms, as shown in Columns 4 and 5 of Table 5.4. India had the highest total GFCE of HK$3.923 trillion, with Maldives recording the lowest total GFCE of HK$10 billion. The PPPs for GFCE were again lower than the exchange rates, with price level indexes (with Hong Kong, China = 100) less than 50 for 15 of the 20 economies (as shown in Column 16 of Table 5.4). These low PLIs were observed despite productivity adjustments made to wages and salaries of government employees as a part of government compensation.

In terms of real GFCE per capita in 2016, Brunei Darussalam had the highest at HK$140,177, which was more than 25 times the regional average of HK$5,447. Nepal had the lowest real GFCE per capita in 2016 (HK$1,634).

Gross Fixed Capital Formation

Gross fixed capital formation (GFCF) is an important component of GDP from a policy perspective. GFCF includes physical infrastructure, such as construction of residential and nonresidential buildings; construction of civil engineering works, such as roads, bridges, railways, ports, and energy networks; and purchases of machinery and equipment. Investments in GFCF are essential to promote an economy's productive

capacity and potential for future growth. High income economies generally invest more into GFCF on a per capita basis.

In 2016, the total GFCF across the 20 participating economies was HK$24.318 trillion in real terms and HK$12.828 trillion in nominal terms (Table 5.5). The PPPs for all economies, except for the reference economy, were less than the corresponding exchange rates, which meant that the PLIs were all less than 100, using Hong Kong, China as the base. India, at HK$10.887 trillion, recorded the highest total GFCF in real terms, while Fiji recorded the lowest with HK$10 billion. Regional GFCF per capita, in real and nominal terms, was HK$10,474 and HK$5,525, respectively. The economy with the highest real GFCF per capita was Brunei Darussalam (HK$143,085), followed by Singapore (HK$134,115) and Hong Kong, China (HK$72,952).

Comparing 2016 Purchasing Power Parities with Extrapolations from 2011

PPPs from an ICP benchmark year can be extrapolated to nonbenchmark years using GDP deflator at the GDP level and using CPI for ICEH by using the conventional method employed in the World Bank's World Development Indicators (WDI) database for extrapolating PPPs with the US dollar as the reference currency. The methodology of extrapolation at aggregate level is described on pages 22 to 24 of this research study. In Table 5.6, the extrapolated PPPs for 2016 from the revised results of ICP's 2011 cycle are compared against the actual PPPs from the 2016 research study. At the GDP level, the ratios of actual to extrapolated PPPs range from 0.90 to 1.13, with the exception of Brunei Darussalam with 1.26. At the ICEH level, the ratios range from 0.88 to 1.12. Although differences can be observed between the actual and extrapolated PPPs, their ratios appear to have no systematic pattern with an average of 1.02 at the GDP level and 1.01 at the ICEH level. The reduced

Table 5.4: Summary Results for Government Final Consumption Expenditure, 2016
(Hong Kong, China as base)

Economy	PPPs (HK$ = 1.00)	Exchange Rates (HK$ = 1.00)	Expenditure (HK$ billion) Based on PPPs	Expenditure (HK$ billion) Based on XRs	Expenditure per Capita (HK$) Based on PPPs	Expenditure per Capita (HK$) Based on XRs	Expenditure per Capita Indexes Asia and the Pacific = 100 Based on PPPs	Based on XRs	HKG = 100 Based on PPPs	Based on XRs	Shares (Asia and the Pacific = 100.00) Expenditure Based on PPPs	Based on XRs	Population	PLIs Asia and the Pacific = 100	HKG=100	Reference Data Population (million)	Expenditure in LCU (billion)
(1)	(2)	(3)	(4)	(5)	(6)	(7)	(8)	(9)	(10)	(11)	(12)	(13)	(14)	(15)	(16)	(17)	(18)
Bangladesh	3.77	10.13	293	109	1,829	681	34	30	5	2	2.31	2.04	6.89	88	37	159.90	1,103
Bhutan	1.75	8.66	14	3	19,716	3,984	362	174	58	12	0.11	0.05	0.03	48	20	0.73	25
Brunei Darussalam	0.07	0.18	59	23	140,177	54,901	2,573	2,392	415	162	0.47	0.44	0.02	93	39	0.42	4
Cambodia	188.81	522.88	36	13	2,374	857	44	37	7	3	0.29	0.25	0.66	86	36	15.25	6,835
Fiji	0.14	0.27	14	7	16,101	8,105	296	353	48	24	0.11	0.13	0.04	119	50	0.87	2
Hong Kong, China	1.00	1.00	248	248	33,799	33,799	621	1,473	100	100	1.96	4.65	0.32	237	100	7.34	248
India	3.88	8.66	3,923	1,760	3,020	1,355	55	59	9	4	31.02	33.02	55.95	106	45	1,299.00	15,234
Indonesia	554.60	1,714.49	2,131	689	8,235	2,664	151	116	24	8	16.85	12.93	11.14	77	32	258.71	1,181,613
Lao People's Democratic Republic	265.13	1,053.72	76	19	11,238	2,828	206	123	33	8	0.60	0.36	0.29	60	25	6.79	20,223
Malaysia	0.24	0.53	639	290	20,184	9,155	371	399	60	27	5.05	5.44	1.36	108	45	31.66	155
Maldives	1.15	1.98	10	6	21,127	12,281	388	535	63	36	0.08	0.11	0.02	138	58	0.47	11
Mongolia	59.26	275.73	59	13	19,142	4,114	351	179	57	12	0.47	0.24	0.13	51	21	3.09	3,504
Nepal	5.61	13.83	46	19	1,634	663	30	29	5	2	0.37	0.35	1.22	96	41	28.39	260
Pakistan	4.87	13.50	707	255	3,619	1,306	66	57	11	4	5.59	4.79	8.42	86	36	195.40	3,443
Philippines	2.95	6.12	548	265	5,309	2,564	97	112	16	8	4.33	4.97	4.45	115	48	103.24	1,620
Singapore	0.14	0.18	321	255	57,192	45,475	1,050	1,981	169	135	2.54	4.78	0.24	189	80	5.61	45
Sri Lanka	3.72	18.76	273	54	12,874	2,552	236	111	38	8	2.16	1.02	0.91	47	20	21.20	1,015
Taipei,China	2.29	4.16	1,077	591	45,788	25,145	841	1,096	135	74	8.52	11.10	1.01	130	55	23.52	2,463
Thailand	1.63	4.55	1,472	527	21,821	7,811	401	340	65	23	11.64	9.89	2.91	85	36	67.46	2,396
Viet Nam	739.53	2,825.86	700	183	7,549	1,976	139	86	22	6	5.53	3.44	3.99	62	26	92.69	517,467
Asia and the Pacific	n.a.	n.a.	12,646	5,329	5,447	2,295	100	100	16	7	100.00	100.00	100.00	100	n.a.	2,321.72	n.a.

HK$ = Hong Kong dollar; HKG = Hong Kong, China; LCU = local currency unit; n.a. = not applicable; PLI = price level index; PPP = purchasing power parity; XR = exchange rate.
Sources: Asian Development Bank estimates (expenditures in local currency units and midyear population estimates were supplied by the economies that participated in the research study). For exchange rates: International Monetary Fund. International Financial Statistics. http://data.imf.org/ (accessed 17 September 2019).

Table 5.5: Summary Results for Gross Fixed Capital Formation, 2016
(Hong Kong, China as base)

Economy	PPPs (HK$ = 1.00)	Exchange Rates (HK$ = 1.00)	Expenditure (HK$ billion)		Expenditure per Capita (HK$)		Expenditure per Capita Indexes				Shares (Asia and the Pacific = 100.00)			PLIs		Reference Data	
			Based on PPPs	Based on XRs	Based on PPPs	Based on XRs	Asia and the Pacific = 100		HKG = 100		Expenditure		Population	Asia and the Pacific = 100	HKG=100	Population (million)	Expenditure in LCU (billion)
							Based on PPPs	Based on XRs	Based on PPPs	Based on XRs	Based on PPPs	Based on XRs					
(1)	(2)	(3)	(4)	(5)	(6)	(7)	(8)	(9)	(10)	(11)	(12)	(13)	(14)	(15)	(16)	(17)	(18)
Bangladesh	5.58	10.13	1,000	551	6,254	3,446	60	62	9	5	4.11	4.30	6.89	104	55	159.90	5,583
Bhutan	4.79	8.66	17	9	23,476	12,992	224	235	32	18	0.07	0.07	0.03	105	55	0.73	82
Brunei Darussalam	0.11	0.18	60	38	143,085	90,620	1,366	1,640	196	124	0.25	0.30	0.02	120	63	0.42	7
Cambodia	289.75	522.88	32	18	2,131	1,181	20	21	3	2	0.13	0.14	0.66	105	55	15.25	9,417
Fiji	0.18	0.27	10	7	11,288	7,738	108	140	15	11	0.04	0.05	0.04	130	69	0.87	2
Hong Kong, China	1.00	1.00	535	535	72,952	72,952	696	1,320	100	100	2.20	4.17	0.32	190	100	7.34	535
India	3.90	8.66	10,887	4,901	8,381	3,773	80	68	11	5	44.77	38.21	55.95	85	45	1,299.00	42,428
Indonesia	847.40	1,714.49	4,768	2,356	18,429	9,109	176	165	25	12	19.61	18.37	11.14	94	49	258.71	4,040,202
Lao People's Democratic Republic	599.23	1,053.72	67	38	9,896	5,628	94	102	14	8	0.28	0.30	0.29	108	57	6.79	40,247
Malaysia	0.53	0.53	1,117	592	35,292	18,688	337	338	48	26	4.59	4.61	1.36	100	53	31.66	316
Maldives	1.66	1.98	15	13	32,790	27,430	313	496	45	38	0.06	0.10	0.02	159	84	0.47	26
Mongolia	180.71	275.73	27	18	8,805	5,771	84	104	12	8	0.11	0.14	0.13	124	66	3.09	4,915
Nepal	7.28	13.83	89	47	3,141	1,652	30	30	4	2	0.37	0.37	1.22	100	53	28.39	649
Pakistan	8.13	13.50	538	324	2,751	1,657	26	30	4	2	2.21	2.52	8.42	114	60	195.40	4,370
Philippines	3.92	6.12	910	583	8,814	5,649	84	102	12	8	3.74	4.55	4.45	121	64	103.24	3,568
Singapore	0.15	0.18	752	648	134,115	115,488	1,280	2,090	184	158	3.09	5.05	0.24	163	86	5.61	115
Sri Lanka	12.13	18.76	262	169	12,355	7,990	118	145	17	11	1.08	1.32	0.91	123	65	21.20	3,177
Taipei,China	3.27	4.16	1,099	862	46,725	36,645	446	663	64	50	4.52	6.72	1.01	149	78	23.52	3,589
Thailand	2.28	4.55	1,472	736	21,815	10,916	208	198	30	15	6.05	5.74	2.91	95	50	67.46	3,348
Viet Nam	1,633.38	2,825.86	660	382	7,125	4,118	68	75	10	6	2.72	2.98	3.99	110	58	92.69	1,078,683
Asia and the Pacific	n.a.	n.a.	24,318	12,828	10,474	5,525	100	100	14	8	100.00	100.00	100.00	100	n.a.	2,321.72	n.a.

HK$ = Hong Kong dollar; HKG = Hong Kong, China; LCU = local currency unit; n.a. = not applicable; PLI = price level index; PPP = purchasing power parity; XR = exchange rate.
Sources: Asian Development Bank estimates (expenditures in local currency units and midyear population estimates were supplied by the economies that participated in the research study). For exchange rates: International Monetary Fund. International Financial Statistics. http://data.imf.org/ (accessed 17 September 2019).

Table 5.6: Ratio of 2016 Purchasing Power Parities to Extrapolations from 2011[a]

Economy	GDP			ICEH		
	Actual 2016 PPP	Extrapolated PPP from 2011[a]	Ratio of Actual to Extrapolated	Actual 2016 PPP	Extrapolated PPP from 2011[a]	Ratio of Actual to Extrapolated
(1)	(2)	(3)	(4)	(5)	(6)	(7)
Bangladesh	4.81	5.36	0.90	4.81	4.98	0.97
Bhutan	3.55	3.67	0.97	3.82	3.58	1.07
Brunei Darussalam	0.11	0.09	1.26	0.11	0.12	0.90
Cambodia	255.51	250.62	1.02	258.29	252.68	1.02
Fiji	0.16	0.18	0.90	0.15	0.17	0.91
Hong Kong, China	1.00	1.00	1.00	1.00	1.00	1.00
India	3.27	3.23	1.01	2.94	3.20	0.92
Indonesia	789.01	712.66	1.11	820.30	749.93	1.09
Lao People's Democratic Republic	506.58	526.10	0.96	547.75	549.57	1.00
Malaysia	0.28	0.26	1.10	0.28	0.26	1.09
Maldives	1.52	1.69	0.90	1.58	1.56	1.01
Mongolia	125.44	114.40	1.10	127.16	125.20	1.02
Nepal	6.11	5.71	1.07	6.12	5.78	1.06
Pakistan	5.91	5.22	1.13	5.66	5.11	1.11
Philippines	3.12	3.25	0.96	2.93	3.08	0.95
Singapore	0.16	0.15	1.07	0.18	0.17	1.06
Sri Lanka	8.83	8.33	1.06	9.24	8.26	1.12
Taipei,China	2.72	2.73	0.99	2.60	2.51	1.04
Thailand	2.13	2.23	0.95	2.12	2.00	1.06
Viet Nam	1,247.01	1,392.68	0.90	1,229.38	1,390.00	0.88

GDP = gross domestic product, ICEH = individual consumption expenditure by households, PPP = purchasing power parity.

[a] 2011 purchasing power parities (PPPs) are revised PPPs based on the comparisons of the 20 economies common between the ICP's 2011 cycle and 2016 research study.

Note: In this table, individual consumption expenditure by households includes expenditure by nonprofit institutions serving households.

Sources: Gross domestic product (GDP) in local currency units and consumer price index were supplied by the participating economies for the International Comparison Program. GDP deflators for Bangladesh, Cambodia, Fiji, India, Malaysia, Maldives, Nepal, and Thailand were sourced from: Asian Development Bank. 2019. Key Indicators for Asia and the Pacific 2019. Manila: Asian Development Bank. GDP deflator for the Lao People's Democratic Republic was derived from: International Monetary Fund. International Financial Statistics. http://data.imf.org/ (accessed 21 January 2020). For Fiji, GDP was rebased to 2011, noting a base year revision and a break in series in 2014. The purchasing power parities used to calculate real GDP are Asian Development Bank estimates.

information approach makes use of comparisons of price data for a subset of comparable items priced in the 2011 benchmark, and at the higher aggregate levels the estimates from it can be considered more robust than conventional extrapolation method.

Conclusions about the Results

The PPP results, based on the reduced information method for Asia and the Pacific in 2016, have similar patterns to those observed for the ICP's 2011 and 2017 cycles. However, caution must be exercised in comparing this study's results with the 2011 and 2017 cycles because the People's Republic of China—the largest economy in the region—and Myanmar did not contribute 2016 data to the study.

For interested users and researchers, there is a wealth of information available from the ICP's 2017 cycle in Asia and the Pacific, in the comprehensive report published in October 2020. The ICP's 2017 cycle covered 22 economies from across the region, with the People's Republic of China and Myanmar taking part. Detailed data from the ICP's 2017 cycle—including PPPs, PPP-based expenditure aggregates, and PLIs for 44 expenditure categories—are provided through online tables and a database (https://icp.adb.org) that can be used to conduct in-depth analyses.

6. Conclusions and Moving Forward

This research study on 2016 purchasing power parities (PPPs) for select economies in Asia and the Pacific was anchored on the reduced information approach, which was also pursued in the study conducted by the Asian Development Bank (ADB) in 2009. Given the enormous resources required to conduct price surveys at the national, regional, and global levels for each cycle of the International Comparison Program (ICP), research is needed to devise reliable methods for updating PPPs in nonbenchmark years, so that these methods are sufficiently less costly than conducting a full-scale benchmark. This was the main motivation of this study which replicated the 2009 methodology with some improvements. While for the household price surveys the same reduced information approach was applied, considering the limitations of this approach to price surveys for gross fixed capital formation and government compensation, full-scale price surveys were implemented. There were several studies in the 1970s and 1980s in this direction, but the issue had not been pursued in more recent decades because the main focus for the ICP was on increasing coverage and participation of economies worldwide—a goal that has been accomplished, with full participation of 177 economies in the ICP's 2011 cycle and 176 economies in its 2017 cycle.

This study on 2016 data, along with the 2009 update, demonstrates that the reduced information approach, which is based on price data collected for only a subset of items, is feasible. Despite this feasibility, however, there are a number aspects of the approach that need to be examined and, more importantly, it is necessary to establish the robustness of the approach when applied at different points in time.

Stability of the Commodity Subsets Selected Using the Combinatorial Approach

The combinatorial approach is designed to pick the best subset of items that will result in basic-heading level PPPs that are closest to the actual PPPs derived using price data supplied by the economies on the full list of items used in an ICP benchmark cycle. This means that the combinatorial approach is sensitive to small changes in the price data provided. It is useful to compare the subsets of items selected as a part of the 2009 and 2016 price collection surveys. The "Rice" basic heading had a total of 20 items in the ICP's 2011 benchmark cycle, of which 19 were common with the 2005 list. The problem was to select the best subset of six items (based on a sampling ratio of 30%) in 2009 and 2016. These were:

2009 Survey: Premium rice #1, Premium rice #3, Premium rice #4, Brown rice, White rice #1, and White rice #2.

2016 Survey: White rice #3, White rice #2, White rice #8; Premium rice #2, Brown rice, and Glutinous rice.

"White rice #2" and "Brown rice" were the only two items common to both 2009 and 2016, even though "Rice" is a basic heading with fairly well-defined products. "Glutinous rice" was an additional item under the "Rice" basic heading in the ICP's 2011 cycle. Price relativities between the other items did not change substantially.

In this regard, it would be useful to also conduct these comparisons for data from the ICP's 2017 cycle, to examine the robustness of the core list of products selected in the basic headings resulting from the combinatorial approach.

Sensitivity of Factors to Adjust Purchasing Power Parities Derived from the Reduced Information Approach

In identifying the products to be priced in 2016, a 30% sample of items (core list) from the ICP's full 2011 product list was selected for each basic heading using a combinatorial approach. This approach assumes that most of the products priced in 2011 were relevant in 2016. While the specifications of many food items may not change significantly between two time periods, specifications for electronic products are likely to change due to rapid changes in technology, changes in models, obsolescence, or entry of new products. For 2016 price collection, the core product list was further refined by excluding obsolete items and including a set of electronic and fast-evolving items.

Efforts were made to ensure that all economies could satisfy the minimum requirement for PPP calculation, i.e., the pricing of at least one product in each basic heading. This was sometimes not possible when the product list had very limited items, or if the items were unrepresentative in some economy, and the result was gaps in pricing. The problem of missing prices for some basic headings, and consequent failure of the country-product-dummy method for any given economy in this research study, meant that it was necessary to undertake gap-filling processes to ensure the connectivity of the price matrix. Under certain scenarios, however, it may not be possible to gap-fill in any meaningful manner. Further, the fewer the number of items in a basic heading (say just one item priced in a basic heading) would increase the size of error. These procedures and their implications need to be explored carefully.

Adjusting basic-heading PPPs based on the reduced information (core list)—determined on the basis of a combinatorial approach and a predetermined proportion to be sampled—to basic-heading PPPs derived using the full list price information is a critical step in the procedure used for the 2009 and 2016 updates. This approach relies on the strong assumption that the adjustment factors, derived using PPPs for the core list and the full list in the ICP's 2011 benchmark year, would still be applicable for 2016. However, the results outlined in Chapter 5 of this report indicate that these adjustment factors may not usually be stable. Tables 6.1 and 6.2 present the adjustment factors for the "Rice" basic heading from the ICP's 2005 and 2011 cycles, which were used for the 2009 and 2016 updates, respectively.

It is important to note that economy participation in the 2009 and 2016 updates was different, with 20 economies common to both years, and with one additional economy (the People's Republic of China - not shown in the table) participating in 2009. Notwithstanding this difference, the adjustment factors for the "Rice" basic heading in Tables 6.1 and 6.2 differ significantly for some economies. For Bhutan, the adjustment in 2016 was +25% compared to +3% in 2009. In the case of Viet Nam, the adjustment was +7% in 2016 compared to -11% in 2009, and for Thailand the adjustment was +7% in 2016 compared to -8% in 2009. For Indonesia, the adjustment factor in 2016 was +5% compared to −16% in 2009.

Differences in the adjustment factors can be observed between Table 4.7 and the corresponding table in the 2009 report (ADB 2012a, 26), although the differences in adjustment factors at the higher levels of aggregates are less pronounced. Such differences however point to the instability in the adjustment factors; an important aspect given that this study's results are influenced by these adjustment factors.

In addition, the price surveys for household consumption items for the ICP's 2011 cycle covered all geographic areas of the participating economies,

Table 6.1: Adjustment Factors for "Rice" Basic Heading, 2005 International Comparison Program Used for 2009 Update
(HK$=1.00)

Basic Heading Code	Basic Heading Description	BAN	BHU	BRU	CAM	FIJ	HKG	IND	INO	LAO	MAL	MLD	MON	NEP	PAK	PHI	SIN	SRI	TAP	THA	VIE
1101111	Rice	1.05	1.03	0.94	1.07	1.11	1.00	1.09	0.84	0.90	1.04	0.91	0.98	0.85	0.87	0.99	1.11	0.90	0.98	0.92	0.89

BAN = Bangladesh; BHU = Bhutan; BRU = Brunei Darussalam; CAM = Cambodia; FIJ = Fiji; HKG = Hong Kong, China; IND = India; INO = Indonesia;
LAO = Lao People's Democratic Republic; MAL = Malaysia; MLD = Maldives; MON = Mongolia; NEP = Nepal; PAK = Pakistan; PHI = Philippines; SIN = Singapore; SRI = Sri Lanka;
TAP = Taipei,China; THA = Thailand; VIE = Viet Nam.
Source: Asian Development Bank estimates for Hong Kong, China = 1.00 calculated from core-to-full ratios available in Asian Development Bank. 2012a. *2009 Purchasing Power Parity Update for Selected Economies in Asia and the Pacific: A Research Study.* Manila. https://www.adb.org/publications/2009-purchasing-power-parity-update-selected-economies-asia-and-pacific-research-study.

Table 6.2: Adjustment Factors for "Rice" Basic Heading, 2011 International Comparison Program Used for 2016 Research Study
(HK$=1.00)

Basic Heading Code	Basic Heading Description	BAN	BHU	BRU	CAM	FIJ	HKG	IND	INO	LAO	MAL	MLD	MON	NEP	PAK	PHI	SIN	SRI	TAP	THA	VIE
1101111	Rice	0.99	1.25	0.99	1.07	1.03	1.00	1.05	1.05	0.94	0.99	1.05	0.97	0.96	0.99	1.11	1.12	0.91	0.98	1.07	1.07

BAN = Bangladesh; BHU = Bhutan; BRU = Brunei Darussalam; CAM = Cambodia; FIJ = Fiji; HKG = Hong Kong, China; IND = India; INO = Indonesia;
LAO = Lao People's Democratic Republic; MAL = Malaysia; MLD = Maldives; MON = Mongolia; NEP = Nepal; PAK = Pakistan; PHI = Philippines; SIN = Singapore; SRI = Sri Lanka;
TAP = Taipei,China; THA = Thailand; VIE = Viet Nam.
Source: Asian Development Bank estimates.

whereas the price surveys in 2016 were limited to the capital city of each economy. This, however, is based on another strong assumption that the 2011 capital-to-national price relationship of individual items selected in the core list are also stable over a long period of time, which may not hold for many fast-growing economies of Asia.

Determining the Percentage to Be Sampled

The 2009 and 2016 updates used a minimum sample of 30% of items from the ICP's full product list in 2005 and 2011, respectively. Obviously, this does not work for basic headings with a small number of items, so a higher percentage is needed in some cases. A more objective criterion to select the size of the item subset could be developed. The best results, i.e., zero deviations, are obtained when 100% of the items are included for pricing. The root mean square error, between the basic-heading level PPPs with full

and core product lists, increases when the percentage of the sample decreases from 100%. An optimal minimum proportion needs to be determined, but this proportion may differ for each basic heading.

Bias versus Reliability

The combinatorial method used to select the core product lists for price surveys relies on reducing the difference between PPPs derived from the full list and those obtained using the reduced list for a basic heading. This approach may, however, result in increasing standard error associated with the estimated PPPs. Decreasing the number of items priced in a basic heading will automatically increase standard errors, while noninclusion of items that are priced in most of the economies in the core list is also likely to increase standard errors. The current approach does not consider the reliability of the estimated PPPs.

Moving Forward

The ICP is a resource-intensive statistical initiative, with the burden of price collection largely borne by the participating economies. Scarce financial and human resources need to be allocated in large volumes to support the participation of economies in the ICP. Overall, while the reduced information approach used in this study (or some modified version of it) can be considered satisfactory for an update, it may not be suitable for a full benchmark cycle because relationships between capital-city prices and those for the rest of an economy—as well as the relationships between PPPs from the core list and those from the full list—may not remain stable and are likely to change over time. However, even with these limitations, the approach is likely to give more reliable estimates than the conventional extrapolation methodology for estimating higher level aggregate for updating PPPs in years between benchmarks. Moreover, extrapolation of other aggregates such as for gross fixed capital formation and government final consumption expenditure are not available using the extrapolation method due to the lack of reliable deflators needed for extrapolation. Reliable PPPs for these aggregates are best estimated by comparing prices of representative list of full range items across economies.

It may also be that the reduced information approach used in this and the earlier 2009 study was being explored to estimate PPPs for years between benchmarks at a time when the ICP was implemented at extended intervals, with the two ICP cycles since 2005 being implemented every 6 six years (2011 and 2017). With the decision of the United Nations Statistical Commission in 2016, the ICP has become a permanent element of the United Nations Statistical Commission's global statistical work program to be implemented every 3 years, and with this the limitations in the availability of more frequent PPPs over time have been substantially resolved.

In Asia and the Pacific, most national statistical offices are expected to participate in the ICP cycles every 3 years. The two main challenges will be: (i) whether the current burden of a full-scale benchmark can be made lighter in terms of survey workload, and (ii) whether reliable PPPs can be produced for years between benchmarks. One possibility to address the second challenge is to use the reduced information approach for the 2 years between each benchmark cycle. There is, however, an inherent practical problem in this solution: the reduced information approach requires identifying a core list of products drawn using combinatorial approach from the ICP's full benchmark product list, for which the availability of the ICP benchmark results is a must. Unfortunately, due to the nature of the ICP, these results are currently available only in the third year following the benchmark year in which the price data are collected. In view of this, it may not be possible to derive a reduced list using combinatorial approach for survey in the two years immediately following the benchmark year. Another alternative is to adopt the rolling price survey approach, which is followed in the Statistical Office of the European Communities (Eurostat) and Organisation for Economic Co-operation and Development comparisons, and has the potential to provide annual PPPs. This approach has also been recommended by the United Nations Statistical Commission (ECOSOC 2016b). Application of the rolling price survey approach will, of course, require consultations within the region and a careful assessment that its logistical, methodological, and data needs are satisfied by economies in Asia and the Pacific.

Notwithstanding the limitations, this study provides lessons and guiding parameters which may be useful in designing the rolling price survey approach, which requires that the price movements in the ICP closely resemble those in the CPI—somewhat analogous to the requirement between core and full product lists in the reduced information approach.

As the regional implementing agency for the ICP in Asia and the Pacific, ADB will continue to examine various alternatives for ICP implementation in the region and will consider solutions that may better suit the needs, statistical capacities, and availability of resources of the region's economies.

Appendixes

Appendix 1: Statistical Tables

The statistical tables in this appendix are results from the research study on the reduced information approach produced by the Asian Development Bank (ADB) as the regional implementing agency for the International Comparison Program (ICP) for Asia and the Pacific. The results are based on 2016 data supplied by the 20 economies that participated in the research study. It may be noted that the sole objective of the research initiative was to implement and explore a methodology (presented in Chapter 4) as an alternative to the conventional methodology of extrapolating PPPs for nonbenchmark years.

The tables include gross domestic product (GDP) and its major aggregates of actual individual consumption by households (AICH); individual consumption expenditure by households (ICEH) and nonprofit institutions serving households (NPISHs); government final consumption expenditure (GFCE), gross fixed capital formation (GFCF); changes in inventories and acquisitions less disposals of valuables; and balance of exports and imports. The shares in GDP within each economy and to Asia and the Pacific region are also presented.

These expenditure aggregates were derived using the Gini-Éltető-Köves-Szulc (GEKS) method. The real expenditure for each aggregate is derived by dividing the nominal expenditures estimated in local currency units by a purchasing power parity (PPP) that is specific to that aggregate, so real expenditure for such an aggregate may not equal the total of its components' real expenditures within an economy. Some PPPs presented are reference PPPs. For the detailed list of reference PPPs, see Appendix 2. When an economy's implementing agency is not able to provide prices for any of the items for any category corresponding to the available GDP expenditures, the regional implementing agency estimates the PPP for this category using gap-filling techniques based on the country-product-dummy approach.

The list of tables is as follows:

Table A1.1   Purchasing Power Parities, 2016 (Hong Kong, China as base)
Table A1.2   Price Level Indexes, 2016 (Hong Kong, China = 100)
Table A1.3   Price Level Indexes, 2016 (Asia and the Pacific = 100)
Table A1.4   Real Expenditure, 2016 (HK$ billion)
Table A1.5   Economy Shares of Real Expenditure to Asia and the Pacific, 2016 (%)
Table A1.6   Real Expenditure Per Capita, 2016 (HK$)
Table A1.7   Real Expenditure Per Capita Index, 2016 (Asia and the Pacific = 100)
Table A1.8   Shares of Nominal Expenditure, 2016 (%)
Table A1.9   Gross Domestic Product, 2016 (local currency unit, billion)

Table A1.1: Purchasing Power Parities, 2016
(Hong Kong, China as base)

Expenditure Category	BAN	BHU	BRU	CAM	FIJ	HKG	IND	INO	LAO	MAL	MLD	MON	NEP	PAK	PHI	SIN	SRI	TAP	THA	VIE
Gross Domestic Product	4.81	3.55	0.11	255.51	0.16	1.00	3.27	789.01	506.58	0.28	1.52	125.44	6.11	5.91	3.12	0.16	8.83	2.72	2.13	1,247.01
Actual Individual Consumption by Households[a]	4.62	3.55	0.11	245.83	0.15	1.00	2.95	782.41	506.43	0.28	1.52	114.77	5.90	5.48	2.90	0.18	8.35	2.57	2.04	1,155.82
Individual Consumption Expenditure by Households[b]	4.81	3.82	0.11	258.29	0.15	1.00	2.94	820.30	547.75	0.28	1.58	127.16	6.12	5.66	2.93	0.18	9.24	2.60	2.12	1,229.38
Food and nonalcoholic beverages	5.38	4.23	0.13	320.54	0.17	1.00	3.77	1,131.78	690.39	0.31	1.44	137.58	7.21	7.10	3.52	0.16	11.50	3.23	2.57	1,479.51
Food	5.36	4.22	0.13	319.10	0.17	1.00	3.75	1,137.86	680.93	0.31	1.43	136.11	7.15	7.04	3.62	0.16	11.51	3.26	2.56	1,460.98
Government Final Consumption Expenditure	3.77	1.75	0.07	188.81	0.14	1.00	3.88	554.60	265.13	0.24	1.15	59.26	5.61	4.87	2.95	0.14	3.72	2.29	1.63	739.53
Gross Fixed Capital Formation	5.58	4.79	0.11	289.75	0.18	1.00	3.90	847.40	599.23	0.28	1.66	180.71	7.28	8.13	3.92	0.15	12.13	3.27	2.28	1,633.38
Machinery and equipment	9.13	9.20	0.19	563.23	0.27	1.00	5.65	1,550.71	1,020.91	0.41	2.28	302.62	10.78	13.54	5.94	0.20	20.33	4.46	4.45	2,707.93
Construction	3.74	2.89	0.08	164.25	0.14	1.00	2.87	528.87	383.69	0.21	1.35	117.53	5.18	5.16	2.82	0.13	7.78	2.75	1.19	1,074.24
Changes in Inventories and Acquisitions Less Disposals of Valuables	5.92	4.74	0.11	320.33	0.20	1.00	4.35	1,003.37	646.26	0.33	1.69	155.71	7.84	7.38	3.78	0.17	12.23	3.06	2.54	1,584.43
Balance of Exports and Imports	10.13	8.66	0.18	522.88	0.27	1.00	8.66	1,714.49	1,053.72	0.53	1.98	275.73	13.83	13.50	6.12	0.18	18.76	4.16	4.55	2,825.86

BAN = Bangladesh; BHU = Bhutan; BRU = Brunei Darussalam; CAM = Cambodia; FIJ = Fiji; HKG = Hong Kong, China; IND = India; INO = Indonesia; LAO = Lao People's Democratic Republic; MAL = Malaysia; MLD = Maldives; MON = Mongolia; NEP = Nepal; PAK = Pakistan; PHI = Philippines; SIN = Singapore; SRI = Sri Lanka; TAP = Taipei,China; THA = Thailand; VIE = Viet Nam.
a Includes individual consumption expenditure by households and expenditure incurred by nonprofit institutions serving households and government on behalf of households.
b Includes expenditure by nonprofit institutions serving households.
Source: Asian Development Bank estimates.

Table A1.2: Price Level Indexes, 2016
(Hong Kong, China = 100)

Expenditure Category	BAN	BHU	BRU	CAM	FIJ	HKG	IND	INO	LAO	MAL	MLD	MON	NEP	PAK	PHI	SIN	SRI	TAP	THA	VIE
Gross Domestic Product	47	41	60	49	59	100	38	46	48	53	77	45	44	44	51	88	47	65	47	44
Actual Individual Consumption by Households[a]	46	41	60	47	56	100	34	46	48	52	77	42	43	41	47	101	45	62	45	41
Individual Consumption Expenditure by Households[b]	47	44	62	49	57	100	34	48	52	53	80	46	44	42	48	103	49	62	47	44
Food and nonalcoholic beverages	53	49	71	61	64	100	44	66	66	58	73	50	52	53	58	87	61	78	57	52
Food	53	49	71	61	63	100	43	66	65	58	72	49	52	52	59	89	61	78	56	52
Government Final Consumption Expenditure	37	20	39	36	50	100	45	32	25	45	58	21	41	36	48	80	20	55	36	26
Gross Fixed Capital Formation	55	55	63	55	69	100	45	49	57	53	84	66	53	60	64	86	65	78	50	58
Machinery and equipment	90	106	105	108	102	100	65	90	97	76	115	110	78	100	97	113	108	107	98	96
Construction	37	33	42	31	52	100	33	31	36	39	68	43	37	38	46	74	42	66	26	38
Changes in Inventories and Acquisitions Less Disposals of Valuables	58	55	64	61	73	100	50	59	61	61	85	56	57	55	62	97	65	74	56	56
Balance of Exports and Imports	100	100	100	100	100	100	100	100	100	100	100	100	100	100	100	100	100	100	100	100

BAN = Bangladesh; BHU = Bhutan; BRU = Brunei Darussalam; CAM = Cambodia; FIJ = Fiji; HKG = Hong Kong, China; IND = India; INO = Indonesia; LAO = Lao People's Democratic Republic; MAL = Malaysia; MLD = Maldives; MON = Mongolia; NEP = Nepal; PAK = Pakistan; PHI = Philippines; SIN = Singapore; SRI = Sri Lanka; TAP = Taipei,China; THA = Thailand; VIE = Viet Nam.
a Includes individual consumption expenditure by households and expenditure incurred by nonprofit institutions serving households and government on behalf of households.
b Includes expenditure by nonprofit institutions serving households.
Source: Asian Development Bank estimates.

Table A1.3: Price Level Indexes, 2016
(Asia and the Pacific = 100)

Expenditure Category	BAN	BHU	BRU	CAM	FIJ	HKG	IND	INO	LAO	MAL	MLD	MON	NEP	PAK	PHI	SIN	SRI	TAP	THA	VIE
Gross Domestic Product	102	88	130	105	127	215	81	99	103	113	165	98	95	94	110	189	101	140	101	95
Actual Individual Consumption by Households[a]	105	95	139	109	129	231	79	106	111	121	178	96	99	94	109	235	103	142	104	95
Individual Consumption Expenditure by Households[b]	108	101	141	113	130	228	77	109	119	122	182	105	101	96	109	234	112	142	106	99
Food and nonalcoholic beverages	101	93	136	117	122	190	83	126	125	110	138	95	99	100	109	166	117	148	108	100
Food	101	93	136	117	120	192	83	127	124	111	138	95	99	100	113	171	118	150	108	99
Government Final Consumption Expenditure	88	48	93	86	119	237	106	77	60	108	138	51	96	86	115	189	47	130	85	62
Gross Fixed Capital Formation	104	105	120	105	130	190	85	94	108	100	159	124	100	114	121	163	123	149	95	110
Machinery and equipment	110	130	128	132	124	122	80	111	118	93	141	134	95	123	119	138	133	131	120	117
Construction	102	92	117	87	143	277	92	85	101	109	188	118	104	106	127	204	115	183	72	105
Changes in Inventories and Acquisitions Less Disposals of Valuables	115	107	126	120	142	196	99	115	120	120	167	111	111	107	121	190	128	144	110	110
Balance of Exports and Imports	100	100	100	100	100	100	100	100	100	100	100	100	100	100	100	100	100	100	100	100

BAN = Bangladesh; BHU = Bhutan; BRU = Brunei Darussalam; CAM = Cambodia; FIJ = Fiji; HKG = Hong Kong, China; IND = India; INO = Indonesia; LAO = Lao People's Democratic Republic; MAL = Malaysia; MLD = Maldives; MON = Mongolia; NEP = Nepal; PAK = Pakistan; PHI = Philippines; SIN = Singapore; SRI = Sri Lanka; TAP = Taipei,China; THA = Thailand; VIE = Viet Nam.
[a] Includes individual consumption expenditure by households and expenditure incurred by nonprofit institutions serving households and government on behalf of households.
[b] Includes expenditure by nonprofit institutions serving households.
Source: Asian Development Bank estimates.

Table A1.4: Real Expenditure, 2016
(HK$ billion)

Expenditure Category	BAN	BHU	BRU	CAM	FIJ	HKG	IND	INO	LAO	MAL	MLD	MON	NEP	PAK	PHI	SIN	SRI	TAP	THA	VIE	AP
Gross Domestic Product	3,856.5	42.0	147.3	318.0	64.6	2,490.6	45,655.6	15,718.1	255.2	4,366.0	44.7	190.9	368.6	5,164.7	4,637.4	2,804.3	1,348.9	6,322.6	6,836.8	3,610.8	104,243.6
Actual Individual Consumption by Households[a]	2,828.4	23.3	41.0	277.9	50.2	1,747.4	31,755.3	9,741.4	144.7	2,690.9	20.7	127.0	334.5	4,740.1	3,949.9	974.1	971.0	4,021.7	4,038.3	2,496.5	70,974.5
Individual Consumption Expenditure by Households[b]	2,656.4	19.8	30.1	249.7	44.5	1,649.9	30,265.8	8,742.6	127.5	2,370.4	17.2	103.3	311.5	4,365.9	3,648.4	875.4	822.3	3,479.4	3,328.5	2,164.2	65,272.9
Food and nonalcoholic beverages	1,230.0	6.2	4.4	91.4	12.9	183.1	7,143.5	1,979.0	43.7	490.9	3.2	29.9	161.4	1,178.8	1,278.4	69.1	194.5	413.9	774.8	581.1	15,870.4
Food	1,231.4	5.9	4.0	87.7	12.4	172.3	7,085.2	1,795.1	39.6	471.8	2.7	27.9	160.5	1,130.6	1,140.7	59.9	191.0	382.2	678.6	566.7	15,246.3
Government Final Consumption Expenditure	292.5	14.3	59.2	36.2	14.0	248.0	3,923.4	2,130.6	76.3	639.0	10.0	59.1	46.4	707.1	548.1	320.7	273.0	1,076.9	1,472.0	699.7	12,646.4
Gross Fixed Capital Formation	1,000.0	17.1	60.5	32.5	9.8	535.2	10,886.7	4,767.8	67.2	1,117.4	15.5	27.2	89.2	537.6	910.0	752.0	262.0	1,099.0	1,471.5	660.4	24,318.3
Machinery and equipment	158.7	2.8	12.3	7.1	4.1	160.5	2,232.4	413.9	12.2	216.1	5.6	3.7	13.1	112.3	217.5	160.8	84.5	328.8	428.9	95.2	4,670.5
Construction	1,081.7	18.9	53.9	28.5	4.0	325.5	7,701.7	5,742.9	45.8	880.3	8.4	21.1	69.7	362.0	637.2	420.9	175.9	459.8	997.2	706.0	19,741.2
Changes in Inventories and Acquisitions Less Disposals of Valuables	0.5	0.2	-2.9	1.8	0.6	0.4	1,291.6	-85.2	-0.0	5.6	0.4	8.0	14.1	66.1	-8.8	11.9	80.9	-8.8	-151.9	82.4	1,307.1
Balance of Exports and Imports	-90.8	-3.9	10.5	-0.2	-1.5	57.0	-323.8	54.7	-1.0	155.5	1.5	4.2	-48.7	-186.0	-220.1	656.7	-46.6	508.3	472.4	40.8	1,039.0

0.0 = magnitude is less than half of unit employed; AP = Asia and the Pacific; BAN = Bangladesh; BHU = Bhutan; BRU = Brunei Darussalam; CAM = Cambodia; FIJ = Fiji; HK$ = Hong Kong dollars; HKG = Hong Kong, China; IND = India; INO = Indonesia; LAO = Lao People's Democratic Republic; MAL = Malaysia; MLD = Maldives; MON = Mongolia; NEP = Nepal; PAK = Pakistan; PHI = Philippines; SIN = Singapore; SRI = Sri Lanka; TAP = Taipei,China; THA = Thailand; VIE = Viet Nam.

Note: Each real aggregate value is derived by using a purchasing power parity that is specific to that aggregate, so real aggregates may not sum to the total of their real components for an economy.

[a] Includes individual consumption expenditure by households and expenditure incurred by nonprofit institutions serving households and government on behalf of households.

[b] Includes expenditure by nonprofit institutions serving households.

Source: Asian Development Bank estimates.

Table A1.5: Economy Shares of Real Expenditure to Asia and the Pacific, 2016
(%)

Expenditure Category	BAN	BHU	BRU	CAM	FIJ	HKG	IND	INO	LAO	MAL	MLD	MON	NEP	PAK	PHI	SIN	SRI	TAP	THA	VIE	AP
Gross Domestic Product	3.70	0.04	0.14	0.31	0.06	2.39	43.80	15.08	0.24	4.19	0.04	0.18	0.35	4.95	4.45	2.69	1.29	6.07	6.56	3.46	100.00
Actual Individual Consumption by Households[a]	3.99	0.03	0.06	0.39	0.07	2.46	44.74	13.73	0.20	3.79	0.03	0.18	0.47	6.68	5.57	1.37	1.37	5.67	5.69	3.52	100.00
Individual Consumption Expenditure by Households[b]	4.07	0.03	0.05	0.38	0.07	2.53	46.37	13.39	0.20	3.63	0.03	0.16	0.48	6.69	5.59	1.34	1.26	5.33	5.10	3.32	100.00
Food and nonalcoholic beverages	7.75	0.04	0.03	0.58	0.08	1.15	45.01	12.47	0.28	3.09	0.02	0.19	1.02	7.43	8.06	0.44	1.23	2.61	4.88	3.66	100.00
Food	8.08	0.04	0.03	0.58	0.08	1.13	46.47	11.77	0.26	3.09	0.02	0.18	1.05	7.42	7.48	0.39	1.25	2.51	4.45	3.72	100.00
Government Final Consumption Expenditure	2.31	0.11	0.47	0.29	0.11	1.96	31.02	16.85	0.60	5.05	0.08	0.47	0.37	5.59	4.33	2.54	2.16	8.52	11.64	5.53	100.00
Gross Fixed Capital Formation	4.11	0.07	0.25	0.13	0.04	2.20	44.77	19.61	0.28	4.59	0.06	0.11	0.37	2.21	3.74	3.09	1.08	4.52	6.05	2.72	100.00
Machinery and equipment	3.40	0.06	0.26	0.15	0.09	3.44	47.80	8.86	0.26	4.63	0.12	0.08	0.28	2.40	4.66	3.44	1.81	7.04	9.18	2.04	100.00
Construction	5.48	0.10	0.27	0.14	0.02	1.65	39.01	29.09	0.23	4.46	0.04	0.11	0.35	1.83	3.23	2.13	0.89	2.33	5.05	3.58	100.00
Changes in Inventories and Acquisitions Less Disposals of Valuables	0.04	0.02	-0.22	0.14	0.05	0.03	98.82	-6.52	-0.00	0.42	0.03	0.61	1.08	5.06	-0.68	0.91	6.19	-0.68	-11.62	6.31	100.00
Balance of Exports and Imports	-8.74	-0.38	1.01	-0.02	-0.14	5.49	-31.17	5.27	-0.10	14.97	0.14	0.40	-4.69	-17.90	-21.19	63.21	-4.49	48.92	45.46	3.93	100.00

0.00 = magnitude is less than half of unit employed; AP = Asia and the Pacific; BAN = Bangladesh; BHU = Bhutan; BRU = Brunei Darussalam; CAM = Cambodia; FIJ = Fiji; HKG = Hong Kong, China; IND = India; INO = Indonesia; LAO = Lao People's Democratic Republic; MAL = Malaysia; MLD = Maldives; MON = Mongolia; NEP = Nepal; PAK = Pakistan; PHI = Philippines; SIN = Singapore; SRI = Sri Lanka; TAP = Taipei,China; THA = Thailand; VIE = Viet Nam.

Note: Each real aggregate value is derived by using a purchasing power parity that is specific to that aggregate, so real aggregates may not sum to the total of their real components for an economy.

a Includes individual consumption expenditure by households and expenditure incurred by nonprofit institutions serving households and government on behalf of households.

b Includes expenditure by nonprofit institutions serving households.

Source: Asian Development Bank estimates.

Table A1.6: Real Expenditure Per Capita, 2016
(HK$)

Expenditure Category	BAN	BHU	BRU	CAM	FIJ	HKG	IND	INO	LAO	MAL	MLD	MON	NEP	PAK	PHI	SIN	SRI	TAP	THA	VIE	AP
Gross Domestic Product	24,118	57,791	348,474	20,851	74,336	339,478	35,147	60,757	37,601	137,901	94,739	61,793	12,983	26,431	44,917	500,134	63,618	268,818	101,354	38,955	44,899
Actual Individual Consumption by Households[a]	17,689	32,124	97,114	18,224	57,689	238,180	24,446	37,654	21,313	84,992	43,919	41,119	11,783	24,259	38,258	173,733	45,796	170,992	59,867	26,934	30,570
Individual Consumption Expenditure by Households[b]	16,613	27,224	71,222	16,375	51,232	224,892	23,299	33,794	18,791	74,868	36,464	33,430	10,971	22,343	35,338	156,134	38,782	147,935	49,344	23,349	28,114
Food and nonalcoholic beverages	7,692	8,477	10,447	5,997	14,824	24,962	5,499	7,650	6,443	15,505	6,761	9,688	5,686	6,033	12,382	12,324	9,174	17,600	11,486	6,269	6,836
Food	7,701	8,074	9,401	5,751	14,314	23,491	5,454	6,939	5,840	14,903	5,792	9,032	5,653	5,786	11,049	10,684	9,010	16,248	10,060	6,114	6,567
Government Final Consumption Expenditure	1,829	19,716	140,177	2,374	16,101	33,799	3,020	8,235	11,238	20,184	21,127	19,142	1,634	3,619	5,309	57,192	12,874	45,788	21,821	7,549	5,447
Gross Fixed Capital Formation	6,254	23,476	143,085	2,131	11,288	72,952	8,381	18,429	9,896	35,292	32,790	8,805	3,141	2,751	8,814	134,115	12,355	46,725	21,815	7,125	10,474
Machinery and equipment	993	3,894	29,019	465	4,759	21,873	1,719	1,600	1,793	6,827	11,922	1,200	462	575	2,107	28,685	3,985	13,981	6,358	1,027	2,012
Construction	6,765	26,033	127,409	1,871	4,572	44,366	5,929	22,199	6,746	27,805	17,881	6,832	2,455	1,852	6,171	75,064	8,294	19,549	14,783	7,616	8,503
Changes in Inventories and Acquisitions Less Disposals of Valuables	3	285	-6,764	119	734	61	994	-329	-0	175	943	2,592	497	338	-86	2,121	3,815	-376	-2,251	889	563
Balance of Exports and Imports	-568	-5,420	24,779	-11	-1,692	7,775	-249	212	-146	4,913	3,171	1,347	-1,715	-952	-2,132	117,128	-2,199	21,611	7,003	440	448

0 = magnitude is less than half of unit employed; AP = Asia and the Pacific; BAN = Bangladesh; BHU = Bhutan; BRU = Brunei Darussalam; CAM = Cambodia; FIJ = Fiji; HK$ = Hong Kong dollars; HKG = Hong Kong, China; IND = India; INO = Indonesia; LAO = Lao People's Democratic Republic; MAL = Malaysia; MLD = Maldives; MON = Mongolia; NEP = Nepal; PAK = Pakistan; PHI = Philippines; SIN = Singapore; SRI = Sri Lanka; TAP = Taipei,China; THA = Thailand; VIE = Viet Nam.

Note: Each real aggregate value is derived by using a purchasing power parity that is specific to that aggregate, so real aggregates may not sum to the total of their real components for an economy.

a Includes individual consumption expenditure by households and expenditure incurred by nonprofit institutions serving households and government on behalf of households.

b Includes expenditure by nonprofit institutions serving households.

Source: Asian Development Bank estimates.

Table A1.7: Real Expenditure Per Capita Index, 2016
(Asia and the Pacific = 100)

Expenditure Category	BAN	BHU	BRU	CAM	FIJ	HKG	IND	INO	LAO	MAL	MLD	MON	NEP	PAK	PHI	SIN	SRI	TAP	THA	VIE	AP
Gross Domestic Product	54	129	776	46	166	756	78	135	84	307	211	138	29	59	100	1,114	142	599	226	87	100
Actual Individual Consumption by Households[a]	58	105	318	60	189	779	80	123	70	278	144	135	39	79	125	568	150	559	196	88	100
Individual Consumption Expenditure by Households[b]	59	97	253	58	182	800	83	120	67	266	130	119	39	79	126	555	138	526	176	83	100
Food and nonalcoholic beverages	113	124	153	88	217	365	80	112	94	227	99	142	83	88	181	180	134	257	168	92	100
Food	117	123	143	88	218	358	83	106	89	227	88	138	86	88	168	163	137	247	153	93	100
Government Final Consumption Expenditure	34	362	2,573	44	296	621	55	151	206	371	388	351	30	66	97	1,050	236	841	401	139	100
Gross Fixed Capital Formation	60	224	1,366	20	108	696	80	176	94	337	313	84	30	26	84	1,280	118	446	208	68	100
Machinery and equipment	49	194	1,443	23	237	1,087	85	80	89	339	593	60	23	29	105	1,426	198	695	316	51	100
Construction	80	306	1,498	22	54	522	70	261	79	327	210	80	29	22	73	883	98	230	174	90	100
Changes in Inventories and Acquisitions Less Disposals of Valuables	1	51	-1,201	21	130	11	177	-58	-0	31	168	460	88	60	-15	377	678	-67	-400	158	100
Balance of Exports and Imports	-127	-1,211	5,537	-2	-378	1,737	-56	47	-33	1,098	709	301	-383	-213	-476	26,173	-491	4,829	1,565	98	100

0 = magnitude is less than half of unit employed; AP = Asia and the Pacific; BAN = Bangladesh; BHU = Bhutan; BRU = Brunei Darussalam; CAM = Cambodia; FIJ = Fiji; HKG = Hong Kong, China; IND = India; INO = Indonesia; LAO = Lao People's Democratic Republic; MAL = Malaysia; MLD = Maldives; MON = Mongolia; NEP = Nepal; PAK = Pakistan; PHI = Philippines; SIN = Singapore; SRI = Sri Lanka; TAP = Taipei,China; THA = Thailand; VIE = Viet Nam.
Note: Each real aggregate value is derived by using a purchasing power parity that is specific to that aggregate, so real aggregates may not sum to the total of their real components for an economy.
[a] Includes individual consumption expenditure by households and expenditure incurred by nonprofit institutions serving households and government on behalf of households.
[b] Includes expenditure by nonprofit institutions serving households.
Source: Asian Development Bank estimates.

Table A1.8: Shares of Nominal Expenditure, 2016
(%)

Expenditure Category	BAN	BHU	BRU	CAM	FIJ	HKG	IND	INO	LAO	MAL	MLD	MON	NEP	PAK	PHI	SIN	SRI	TAP	THA	VIE	AP
Gross Domestic Product	100.00	100.00	100.00	100.00	100.00	100.00	100.00	100.00	100.00	100.00	100.00	100.00	100.00	100.00	100.00	100.00	100.00	100.00	100.00	100.00	100.00
Actual Individual Consumption by Households[a]	70.39	55.49	27.91	84.09	73.43	70.16	62.65	61.46	56.66	61.08	46.52	60.88	87.61	85.13	78.98	40.04	68.11	60.07	56.53	64.08	63.33
Individual Consumption Expenditure by Households[b]	68.89	50.61	20.95	79.39	66.61	66.25	59.53	57.83	54.04	54.83	39.91	54.84	84.62	81.01	73.71	36.38	63.83	52.60	48.43	59.09	59.03
Food and nonalcoholic beverages	35.71	17.45	3.55	36.08	21.68	7.35	18.04	18.06	23.35	12.35	6.76	17.20	51.64	27.43	31.06	2.45	18.79	7.78	13.70	19.09	17.21
Food	35.57	16.60	3.19	34.44	20.35	6.92	17.78	16.47	20.88	11.86	5.75	15.86	50.94	26.10	28.48	2.17	18.46	7.26	11.91	18.39	16.42
Government Final Consumption Expenditure	5.95	16.80	26.15	8.41	18.43	9.96	10.19	9.53	15.64	12.58	16.89	14.63	11.55	11.29	11.19	10.33	8.52	14.34	16.46	11.49	10.99
Gross Fixed Capital Formation	30.11	54.79	43.17	11.59	17.59	21.49	28.39	32.58	31.13	25.69	37.73	20.53	28.80	14.33	24.64	26.23	26.69	20.90	23.01	23.96	26.46
Machinery and equipment	7.81	17.45	14.50	4.92	10.99	6.44	8.44	5.18	9.61	7.15	18.88	4.68	6.27	4.98	8.92	7.37	14.43	8.54	13.12	5.72	7.88
Construction	21.80	36.60	25.63	5.77	5.39	13.07	14.77	24.49	13.59	15.08	16.74	10.36	16.02	6.13	12.39	12.58	11.50	7.36	8.14	16.84	14.73
Changes in Inventories and Acquisitions Less Disposals of Valuables	0.02	0.66	-2.08	0.72	1.21	0.02	3.76	-0.69	-0.00	0.15	1.11	5.21	4.91	1.60	-0.23	0.47	8.31	-0.16	-2.65	2.90	1.37
Balance of Exports and Imports	-4.96	-22.86	11.80	-0.11	-3.85	2.29	-1.88	0.76	-0.81	6.75	4.36	4.79	-29.89	-8.23	-9.30	26.60	-7.34	12.32	14.76	2.56	2.14

0.00 = magnitude is less than half of unit employed; AP = Asia and the Pacific; BAN = Bangladesh; BHU = Bhutan; BRU = Brunei Darussalam; CAM = Cambodia; FIJ = Fiji; HKG = Hong Kong, China; IND = India; INO = Indonesia; LAO = Lao People's Democratic Republic; MAL = Malaysia; MLD = Maldives; MON = Mongolia; NEP = Nepal; PAK = Pakistan; PHI = Philippines; SIN = Singapore; SRI = Sri Lanka; TAP = Taipei,China; THA = Thailand; VIE = Viet Nam.
[a] Includes individual consumption expenditure by households and expenditure incurred by nonprofit institutions serving households and government on behalf of households.
[b] Includes expenditure by nonprofit institutions serving households.
Source: Asian Development Bank estimates.

Table A1.9: Gross Domestic Product, 2016
(local currency unit, billion)

Expenditure Category	BAN	BHU	BRU	CAM	FIJ	HKG	IND	INO	LAO	MAL	MLD	MON	NEP	PAK	PHI	SIN	SRI	TAP	THA	VIE
Gross Domestic Product	18,543.39	149.15	15.79	81,241.90	10.32	2,490.62	149,451.84	12,401,728.50	129,279.12	1,231.02	67.84	23,942.86	2,253.16	30,498.97	14,480.35	439.41	11,906.75	17,176.30	14,554.57	4,502,732.99
Actual Individual Consumption by Households[a]	13,053.53	82.76	4.41	68,317.15	7.58	1,747.43	93,634.13	7,621,742.65	73,254.83	751.91	31.56	14,577.25	1,974.07	25,964.84	11,436.59	175.96	8,109.10	10,317.48	8,227.83	2,885,539.85
Individual Consumption Expenditure by Households[b]	12,774.18	75.48	3.31	64,495.17	6.87	1,649.94	88,970.89	7,171,522.84	69,856.91	674.96	27.08	13,130.52	1,906.69	24,707.55	10,672.80	159.85	7,599.81	9,034.47	7,048.20	2,660,661.85
Food and nonalcoholic beverages	6,622.56	26.03	0.56	29,310.95	2.24	183.14	26,963.91	2,239,824.06	30,187.81	152.08	4.58	4,117.06	1,163.43	8,366.32	4,498.26	10.74	2,237.72	1,337.02	1,993.36	859,763.00
Food	6,595.22	24.75	0.50	27,981.85	2.10	172.34	26,579.93	2,042,582.83	26,989.24	146.05	3.90	3,797.32	1,147.69	7,960.26	4,124.70	9.52	2,198.16	1,246.92	1,734.00	827,927.00
Government Final Consumption Expenditure	1,102.88	25.06	4.13	6,835.45	1.90	247.97	15,233.95	1,181,613.14	20,222.61	154.90	11.46	3,503.72	260.35	3,443.47	1,619.64	45.38	1,014.75	2,462.92	2,395.97	517,467.00
Gross Fixed Capital Formation	5,583.37	81.72	6.82	9,416.75	1.82	535.22	42,427.76	4,040,201.81	40,247.26	316.21	25.60	4,915.10	648.93	4,370.25	3,568.23	115.25	3,177.37	3,589.30	3,348.31	1,078,683.30
Machinery and equipment	1,449.12	26.02	2.29	3,995.45	1.13	160.47	12,606.39	641,847.38	12,425.00	88.07	12.81	1,121.33	141.24	1,520.14	1,291.38	32.37	1,717.86	1,466.73	1,909.41	257,687.00
Construction	4,042.18	54.59	4.05	4,684.87	0.56	325.09	22,077.34	3,037,239.85	17,568.45	185.69	11.35	2,480.44	361.00	1,868.66	1,794.02	55.26	1,368.93	1,264.20	1,184.53	758,366.00
Changes in Inventories and Acquisitions Less Disposals of Valuables	3.13	0.98	-0.33	582.64	0.13	0.45	5,622.61	-85,446.46	-0.06	1.81	0.75	1,246.54	110.67	487.98	-33.40	2.05	989.11	-27.11	-385.80	130,578.82
Balance of Exports and Imports	-920.16	-34.09	1.86	-88.11	-0.40	57.04	-2,803.37	93,837.17	-1,047.60	83.13	2.96	1,146.98	-673.48	-2,510.28	-1,346.92	116.89	-874.29	2,116.72	2,147.89	115,342.01

BAN = Bangladesh; BHU = Bhutan; BRU = Brunei Darussalam; CAM = Cambodia; FIJ = Fiji; HKG = Hong Kong, China; IND = India; INO = Indonesia; LAO = Lao People's Democratic Republic; MAL = Malaysia; MLD = Maldives; MON = Mongolia; NEP = Nepal; PAK = Pakistan; PHI = Philippines; SIN = Singapore; SRI = Sri Lanka; TAP = Taipei,China; THA = Thailand; VIE = Viet Nam.

Note: Expenditure aggregates presented are the best possible estimates provided by the participating economies, using most recent available data sources, and some of these aggregates may be different from the published expenditure estimates by the economies.

[a] Includes individual consumption expenditure by households and expenditure incurred by nonprofit institutions serving households and government on behalf of households.

[b] Includes expenditure by nonprofit institutions serving households.

Source: Economy sources.

Appendix 2: List of Reference Purchasing Power Parities Used

Code	Description	Reference
1100000	Individual Consumption Expenditure by Households	
1102311	Narcotics	Tobacco
1104A	Actual and imputed rentals for housing	Volume relatives of individual consumption expenditures by households
1104421	Miscellaneous services relating to the dwelling	Maintenance and repair of dwelling Water supply
1105131	Repair of furniture, furnishings, and floor coverings	Maintenance and repair of dwelling
1105331	Repair of household appliances	Maintenance and repair of dwelling
1105511	Major tools and equipment	Major household appliances whether electric or not Small electric household appliances Small tools and miscellaneous accessories
1105622	Household services	Maintenance and repair of dwelling
1106311	Hospital services	Medical services Dental services Paramedical services
1107141	Animal drawn vehicles	Bicycles
1107351	Combined passenger transport	Fuels and lubricants for personal transport equipment Maintenance and repair of personal transport equipment Other services in respect of personal transport equipment Passenger transport by railway Passenger transport by road Passenger transport by air Passenger transport by sea and inland waterway
1109211	Major durables for outdoor and indoor recreation	Bicycles Audiovisual, photographic, and information-processing equipment Recording media Repair of audiovisual, photographic, and information-processing equipment
1109231	Maintenance and repair of other major durables for recreation and culture	Maintenance and repair of personal transport equipment Repair of audiovisual, photographic, and information-processing equipment
1109431	Games of chance	Recreational and sporting services
1112211	Prostitution	PPP for ICEH (110000), excluding health and education basic headings and basic headings with reference PPPs
1112411	Social protection	Compensation of employees from health and education services
1112511	Insurance	PPP for ICEH (110000), excluding health and education basic headings and basic headings with reference PPPs
1112611	Financial intermediation services indirectly measured	PPP for ICEH (110000), excluding health and education basic headings and basic headings with reference PPPs
1112621	Other financial services n.e.c.	PPP for ICEH (110000), excluding health and education basic headings and basic headings with reference PPPs
1112711	Other services n.e.c.	PPP for ICEH (110000), excluding health and education basic headings and basic headings with reference PPPs
1113111	Net purchases abroad	Exchange rates
1200000	Individual Consumption Expenditure by NPISHs	
1201111	Housing - NPISHs	Actual and imputed rentals for housing
1202111	Health - NPISHs	Compensation of employees from production of health services
1203111	Recreation and culture - NPISHs	Cultural services Recreational and sporting services
1204111	Education - NPISHs	Compensation of employees from production of education services
1205111	Social protection and other services - NPISHs	Compensation of employees from production of health and education services
1300000	Individual Consumption Expenditure by Government	
1301111	Housing	Actual and imputed rents
1302111	Pharmaceutical products	Pharmaceutical products (HHC)
1302112	Other medical products	Other medical products (HHC)
1302113	Therapeutic appliances and equipment	Therapeutic appliances and equipment (HHC)
1302121	Outpatient medical services	Medical services (HHC)
1302122	Outpatient dental services	Dental services (HHC)
1302123	Outpatient paramedical services	Paramedical services (HHC)
1302124	Hospital services	Hospital services (HHC)
1302221	Intermediate consumption	PPP for ICEH (110000), excluding basic headings with reference PPPs
1302231	Gross operating surplus	PPP for GFCF (150000), excluding basic headings with reference PPPs
1302241	Net taxes on production	Compensation of employees from production of health services
1302251	Receipts from sales	Compensation of employees from production of health services
1303111	Recreation and culture	Cultural services Recreational and sporting services
1304111	Education benefits and reimbursements	Education (1110000)
1304221	Intermediate consumption	PPP for ICEH (110000), excluding basic headings with reference PPPs
1304231	Gross operating surplus	PPP for GFCF (150000), excluding basic headings with reference PPPs

continued on next page

Appendix 2 continued

Code	Description	Reference
1304241	Net taxes on production	Compensation of employees from production of education services
1304251	Receipt from sales	Compensation of employees from production of education services
1305111	Social protection	Compensation of employees from production of health and education services
1400000	**Collective Consumption Expenditure by Government**	
1401121	Intermediate consumption	PPP for ICEH (110000), excluding basic headings with reference PPPs
1401131	Gross operating surplus	PPP for GFCF (150000), excluding basic headings with reference PPPs
1401141	Net taxes on production	Compensation of employees from production of collective services
1401151	Receipts from sales	Compensation of employees from production of collective services
1500000	**Gross Capital Formation**	
1501122	Other transport equipment	Road transport equipment
1501311	Other products	Electrical and optical equipment General purpose machinery Special purpose machinery Road transport equipment
1502111	Changes in inventories	Referenced to basic headings classified as containing predominantly goods, excluding basic headings with reference PPPs
1503111	Acquisitions less disposals of valuables	Exchange rates
1600000	**Balance of Exports and Imports**	
1601111	Exports of goods and services	Exchange rates
1601112	Imports of goods and services	Exchange rates

GFCF = gross fixed capital formation, HHC = household consumption, ICEH = individual consumption expenditure by households, n.e.c. = not elsewhere classified, NPISHs = nonprofit institutions serving households, PPP = purchasing power parity.
Note: The reference PPPs used in the research study on 2016 data are the same as those used in the International Comparison Program's 2017 and 2011 revised results.
Source: Based on International Comparison Program Inter-Agency Coordination Group meeting (23–25 October 2019) and recommendations from the 2017 International Comparison Program Technical Advisory Group.

Appendix 3: International Comparison Program Expenditure Classifications Used

Code	Name	Expenditure Level
1000000	Gross Domestic Product	GDP
1100000	Individual Consumption Expenditure by Households	Main Aggregate
1101000	Food and nonalcoholic beverages	Category
1101100	Food	Group
1101110	Bread and cereals	Class
1101111	Rice	Basic Heading
1101112	Other cereals, flour, and other cereal products	Basic Heading
1101113	Bread	Basic Heading
1101114	Other bakery products	Basic Heading
1101115	Pasta products and couscous	Basic Heading
1101120	Meat	Class
1101121	Beef and veal	Basic Heading
1101122	Pork	Basic Heading
1101123	Lamb, mutton, and goat	Basic Heading
1101124	Poultry	Basic Heading
1101125	Other meats and meat preparations	Basic Heading
1101130	Fish and seafood	Class
1101131	Fresh, chilled, or frozen fish and seafood	Basic Heading
1101132	Preserved or processed fish and seafood	Basic Heading
1101140	Milk, cheese, and eggs	Class
1101141	Fresh milk	Basic Heading
1101142	Preserved milk and other milk products	Basic Heading
1101143	Cheese and curd	Basic Heading
1101144	Eggs and egg-based products	Basic Heading
1101150	Oils and fats	Class
1101151	Butter and margarine	Basic Heading
1101153	Other edible oils and fats	Basic Heading
1101160	Fruit	Class
1101161	Fresh or chilled fruit	Basic Heading
1101162	Frozen, preserved, or processed fruit and fruit-based products	Basic Heading
1101170	Vegetables	Class
1101171	Fresh or chilled vegetables, other than potatoes and other tuber vegetables	Basic Heading
1101172	Fresh or chilled potatoes and other tuber vegetables	Basic Heading
1101173	Frozen, preserved, or processed vegetables and vegetable-based products	Basic Heading
1101180	Sugar, jam, honey, chocolate, and confectionery	Class
1101181	Sugar	Basic Heading
1101182	Jams, marmalades, and honey	Basic Heading
1101183	Confectionery, chocolate, and ice cream	Basic Heading
1101190	Food products n.e.c.	Class
1101191	Food products n.e.c.	Basic Heading
1101200	Nonalcoholic beverages	Group
1101210	Coffee, tea, and cocoa	Class
1101211	Coffee, tea, and cocoa	Basic Heading
1101220	Mineral waters, soft drinks, fruit and vegetable juices	Class
1101221	Mineral waters, soft drinks, fruit and vegetable juices	Basic Heading
1102000	Alcoholic beverages, tobacco, and narcotics	Category
1102100	Alcoholic beverages	Group
1102110	Spirits	Class
1102111	Spirits	Basic Heading
1102120	Wine	Class
1102121	Wine	Basic Heading
1102130	Beer	Class
1102131	Beer	Basic Heading
1102200	Tobacco	Group
1102210	Tobacco	Class
1102211	Tobacco	Basic Heading
1102300	Narcotics	Group
1102310	Narcotics	Class
1102311	Narcotics[a]	Basic Heading
1103000	Clothing and footwear	Category
1103100	Clothing	Group
1103110	Clothing materials, other articles of clothing, and clothing accessories	Class
1103111	Clothing materials, other articles of clothing, and clothing accessories	Basic Heading
1103120	Garments	Class
1103121	Garments	Basic Heading

continued on next page

Appendix 3 continued

Code	Name	Expenditure Level
1103140	Cleaning, repair and hire of clothing	Class
1103141	Cleaning, repair and hire of clothing	Basic Heading
1103200	Footwear	Group
1103210	Shoes and other footwear	Class
1103211	Shoes and other footwear	Basic Heading
1103220	Repair and hire of footwear	Class
1103221	Repair and hire of footwear	Basic Heading
1104000	Housing, water, electricity, gas, and other fuels	Category
1104a	Actual and imputed rentals for housing[c]	Group
1104a	Actual and imputed rentals for housing[c]	Class
1104a	Actual and imputed rentals for housing[c]	Basic Heading
1104300	Maintenance and repair of the dwelling	Group
1104310	Maintenance and repair of the dwelling	Class
1104311	Maintenance and repair of the dwelling	Basic Heading
1104400	Water supply and miscellaneous services relating to the dwelling	Group
1104410	Water supply	Class
1104411	Water supply	Basic Heading
1104420	Miscellaneous services relating to the dwelling	Class
1104421	Miscellaneous services relating to the dwelling[a]	Basic Heading
1104500	Electricity, gas, and other fuels	Group
1104510	Electricity	Class
1104511	Electricity	Basic Heading
1104520	Gas	Class
1104521	Gas	Basic Heading
1104530	Other fuels	Class
1104531	Other fuels	Basic Heading
1105000	Furnishings, household equipment, and routine household maintenance	Category
1105100	Furniture and furnishings, carpets and other floor coverings	Group
1105110	Furniture and furnishings	Class
1105111	Furniture and furnishings	Basic Heading
1105120	Carpets and other floor coverings	Class
1105121	Carpets and other floor coverings	Basic Heading
1105130	Repair of furniture, furnishings, and floor coverings	Class
1105131	Repair of furniture, furnishings, and floor coverings[a]	Basic Heading
1105200	Household textiles	Group
1105210	Household textiles	Class
1105211	Household textiles	Basic Heading
1105300	Household appliances	Group
1105310	Major household appliances, whether electric or not	Class
1105311	Major household appliances, whether electric or not	Basic Heading
1105320	Small electric household appliances	Class
1105321	Small electric household appliances	Basic Heading
1105330	Repair of household appliances	Class
1105331	Repair of household appliances[a]	Basic Heading
1105400	Glassware, tableware, and household utensils	Group
1105410	Glassware, tableware, and household utensils	Class
1105411	Glassware, tableware, and household utensils	Basic Heading
1105500	Tools and equipment for house and garden	Group
1105510	Major tools and equipment	Class
1105511	Major tools and equipment[a]	Basic Heading
1105520	Small tools and miscellaneous accessories	Class
1105521	Small tools and miscellaneous accessories	Basic Heading
1105600	Goods and services for routine household maintenance	Group
1105610	Nondurable household goods	Class
1105611	Nondurable household goods	Basic Heading
1105620	Domestic services and household services	Class
1105621	Domestic services	Basic Heading
1105622	Household services[a]	Basic Heading
1106000	Health	Category
1106100	Medical products, appliances, and equipment	Group
1106110	Pharmaceutical products	Class
1106111	Pharmaceutical products	Basic Heading
1106120	Other medical products	Class
1106121	Other medical products	Basic Heading
1106130	Therapeutic appliances and equipment	Class

continued on next page

Appendix 3 continued

Code	Name	Expenditure Level
1106131	Therapeutic appliances and equipment	Basic Heading
1106200	Outpatient services	Group
1106210	Medical services	Class
1106211	Medical services	Basic Heading
1106220	Dental services	Class
1106221	Dental services	Basic Heading
1106230	Paramedical services	Class
1106231	Paramedical services	Basic Heading
1106300	Hospital services	Group
1106310	Hospital services	Class
1106311	Hospital services[a]	Basic Heading
1107000	Transport	Category
1107100	Purchase of vehicles	Group
1107110	Motor cars	Class
1107111	Motor cars	Basic Heading
1107120	Motor cycles	Class
1107121	Motor cycles	Basic Heading
1107130	Bicycles	Class
1107131	Bicycles	Basic Heading
1107140	Animal drawn vehicles	Class
1107141	Animal drawn vehicles[a]	Basic Heading
1107200	Operation of personal transport equipment	Group
1107220	Fuels and lubricants for personal transport equipment	Class
1107221	Fuels and lubricants for personal transport equipment	Basic Heading
1107230	Maintenance and repair of personal transport equipment	Class
1107231	Maintenance and repair of personal transport equipment	Basic Heading
1107240	Other services in respect of personal transport equipment	Class
1107241	Other services in respect of personal transport equipment	Basic Heading
1107300	Transport services	Group
1107310	Passenger transport by railway	Class
1107311	Passenger transport by railway	Basic Heading
1107320	Passenger transport by road	Class
1107321	Passenger transport by road	Basic Heading
1107330	Passenger transport by air	Class
1107331	Passenger transport by air	Basic Heading
1107340	Passenger transport by sea and inland waterway	Class
1107341	Passenger transport by sea and inland waterway	Basic Heading
1107350	Combined passenger transport	Class
1107351	Combined passenger transport[a]	Basic Heading
1107360	Other purchased transport services	Class
1107361	Other purchased transport services	Basic Heading
1108000	Communication	Category
1108100	Postal services	Group
1108110	Postal services	Class
1108111	Postal services	Basic Heading
1108200	Telephone and telefax equipment	Group
1108210	Telephone and telefax equipment	Class
1108211	Telephone and telefax equipment	Basic Heading
1108300	Telephone and telefax services	Group
1108310	Telephone and telefax services	Class
1108311	Telephone and telefax services	Basic Heading
1109000	Recreation and culture	Category
1109100	Audiovisual, photographic, and information-processing equipment	Group
1109110	Audiovisual, photographic, and information-processing equipment	Class
1109111	Audiovisual, photographic, and information-processing equipment	Basic Heading
1109140	Recording media	Class
1109141	Recording media	Basic Heading
1109150	Repair of audiovisual, photographic, and information-processing equipment	Class
1109151	Repair of audiovisual, photographic, and information-processing equipment	Basic Heading
1109200	Other major durables for recreation and culture	Group
1109210	Major durables for outdoor and indoor recreation	Class
1109211	Major durables for outdoor and indoor recreation[a]	Basic Heading
1109230	Maintenance and repair of other major durables for recreation and culture	Class
1109231	Maintenance and repair of other major durables for recreation and culture[a]	Basic Heading
1109300	Other recreational items and equipment, gardens, and pets	Group

continued on next page

Appendix 3 continued

Code	Name	Expenditure Level
1109310	Other recreational items and equipment	Class
1109311	Other recreational items and equipment	Basic Heading
1109330	Gardens and pets	Class
1109331	Gardens and pets	Basic Heading
1109350	Veterinary and other services for pets	Class
1109351	Veterinary and other services for pets	Basic Heading
1109400	Recreational and cultural services	Group
1109410	Recreational and sporting services	Class
1109411	Recreational and sporting services	Basic Heading
1109420	Cultural services	Class
1109421	Cultural services	Basic Heading
1109430	Games of chance	Class
1109431	Games of chance[a]	Basic Heading
1109500	Newspapers, books, and stationery	Group
1109510	Newspapers, books, and stationery	Class
1109511	Newspapers, books, and stationery	Basic Heading
1109600	Package holidays	Group
1109610	Package holidays	Class
1109611	Package holidays	Basic Heading
1110000	Education	Category
1110100	Education	Group
1110110	Education	Class
1110111	Education	Basic Heading
1111000	Restaurants and hotels	Category
1111100	Catering services	Group
1111110	Catering services	Class
1111111	Catering services	Basic Heading
1111200	Accommodation services	Group
1111210	Accommodation services	Class
1111211	Accommodation services	Basic Heading
1112000	Miscellaneous goods and services	Category
1112100	Personal care	Group
1112110	Hairdressing salons and personal grooming establishments	Class
1112111	Hairdressing salons and personal grooming establishments	Basic Heading
1112120	Appliances, articles, and products for personal care	Class
1112121	Appliances, articles, and products for personal care	Basic Heading
1112200	Prostitution	Group
1112210	Prostitution	Class
1112211	Prostitution[a]	Basic Heading
1112300	Personal effects n.e.c.	Group
1112310	Jewellery, clocks, and watches	Class
1112311	Jewellery, clocks, and watches	Basic Heading
1112320	Other personal effects	Class
1112321	Other personal effects	Basic Heading
1112400	Social protection	Group
1112410	Social protection	Class
1112411	Social protection[a]	Basic Heading
1112500	Insurance	Group
1112510	Insurance	Class
1112511	Insurance[a]	Basic Heading
1112600	Financial services n.e.c.	Group
1112610	Financial intermediation services indirectly measured	Class
1112611	Financial intermediation services indirectly measured[a]	Basic Heading
1112620	Other financial services n.e.c.	Class
1112621	Other financial services n.e.c.[a]	Basic Heading
1112700	Other services n.e.c.	Group
1112710	Other services n.e.c.	Class
1112711	Other services n.e.c.[a]	Basic Heading
1113000	Net purchases abroad	Category
1113100	Net purchases abroad	Group
1113110	Net purchases abroad	Class
1113111	Net purchases abroad[a]	Basic Heading
1200000	Individual Consumption Expenditure by NPISHs	Main Aggregate
1201000	Housing	Category
1201100	Housing	Group

continued on next page

Appendix 3 continued

Code	Name	Expenditure Level
1201110	Housing	Class
1201111	Housing[a]	Basic Heading
1202000	Health	Category
1202100	Health	Group
1202110	Health	Class
1202111	Health[a]	Basic Heading
1203000	Recreation and culture	Category
1203100	Recreation and culture	Group
1203110	Recreation and culture	Class
1203111	Recreation and culture[a]	Basic Heading
1204000	Education	Category
1204100	Education	Group
1204110	Education	Class
1204111	Education[a]	Basic Heading
1205000	Social protection and other services	Category
1205100	Social protection and other services	Group
1205110	Social protection and other services	Class
1205111	Social protection and other services[a]	Basic Heading
1300000	Individual Consumption Expenditure by Government	Main Aggregate
1301000	Housing	Category
1301100	Housing	Group
1301110	Housing	Class
1301111	Housing[a]	Basic Heading
1302000	Health	Category
1302100	Health benefits and reimbursements	Group
1302110	Medical products, appliances, and equipment	Class
1302111	Pharmaceutical products[a]	Basic Heading
1302112	Other medical products[a]	Basic Heading
1302113	Therapeutic appliances and equipment[a]	Basic Heading
1302120	Health services	Class
1302121	Outpatient medical services[a]	Basic Heading
1302122	Outpatient dental services[a]	Basic Heading
1302123	Outpatient paramedical services[a]	Basic Heading
1302124	Hospital services[a]	Basic Heading
1302200	Production of health services	Group
1302210	Compensation of employees	Class
1302211	Compensation of employees	Basic Heading
1302220	Intermediate consumption	Class
1302221	Intermediate consumption[a]	Basic Heading
1302230	Gross operating surplus	Class
1302231	Gross operating surplus[a]	Basic Heading
1302240	Net taxes on production	Class
1302241	Net taxes on production[a]	Basic Heading
1302250	Receipts from sales	Class
1302251	Receipts from sales[a]	Basic Heading
1303000	Recreation and culture	Category
1303100	Recreation and culture	Group
1303110	Recreation and culture	Class
1303111	Recreation and culture[a]	Basic Heading
1304000	Education	Category
1304100	Education benefits and reimbursements	Group
1304110	Education benefits and reimbursements	Class
1304111	Education benefits and reimbursements[a]	Basic Heading
1304200	Production of education services	Group
1304210	Compensation of employees	Class
1304211	Compensation of employees	Basic Heading
1304220	Intermediate consumption	Class
1304221	Intermediate consumption[a]	Basic Heading
1304230	Gross operating surplus	Class
1304231	Gross operating surplus[a]	Basic Heading
1304240	Net taxes on production	Class
1304241	Net taxes on production[a]	Basic Heading
1304250	Receipts from sales	Class
1304251	Receipt from sales[a]	Basic Heading
1305000	Social protection	Category

continued on next page

Appendix 3 continued

Code	Name	Expenditure Level
1305100	Social protection	Group
1305110	Social protection	Class
1305111	Social protection[a]	Basic Heading
1400000	**Collective Consumption Expenditure by Government**	**Main Aggregate**
1401000	Collective services	Category
1401100	Collective services	Group
1401110	Compensation of employees	Class
1401111	Compensation of employees	Basic Heading
1401120	Intermediate consumption	Class
1401121	Intermediate consumption[a]	Basic Heading
1401130	Gross operating surplus	Class
1401131	Gross operating surplus[a]	Basic Heading
1401140	Net taxes on production	Class
1401141	Net taxes on production[a]	Basic Heading
1401150	Receipts from sales	Class
1401151	Receipts from sales[a]	Basic Heading
1500000	**Gross Capital Formation**	**Main Aggregate**
1501000	Gross fixed capital formation	Category
1501100	Machinery and equipment	Group
1501110	Metal products and equipment	Class
1501111	Fabricated metal products, except machinery and equipment	Basic Heading
1501112	Electrical and optical equipment	Basic Heading
1501115	General purpose machinery	Basic Heading
1501116	Special purpose machinery	Basic Heading
1501120	Transport equipment	Class
1501121	Road transport equipment	Basic Heading
1501122	Other transport equipment[a]	Basic Heading
1501200	Construction	Group
1501210	Residential buildings	Class
1501211	Residential buildings[b]	Basic Heading
1501220	Nonresidential buildings	Class
1501221	Nonresidential buildings[b]	Basic Heading
1501230	Civil engineering works	Class
1501231	Civil engineering works[b]	Basic Heading
1501300	Other products	Group
1501310	Other products	Class
1501311	Other products[a]	Basic Heading
1502000	Changes in inventories	Category
1502100	Changes in inventories	Group
1502110	Changes in inventories	Class
1502111	Changes in inventories[a]	Basic Heading
1503000	Acquisitions less disposals of valuables	Category
1503100	Acquisitions less disposals of valuables	Group
1503110	Acquisitions less disposals of valuables	Class
1503111	Acquisitions less disposals of valuables[a]	Basic Heading
1600000	**Balance of Exports and Imports**	**Main Aggregate**
1601000	Balance of exports and imports	Category
1601100	Balance of exports and imports	Group
1601110	Balance of exports and imports	Class
1601111	Exports of goods and services[a]	Basic Heading
1601112	Imports of goods and services[a]	Basic Heading

GDP = gross domestic product, n.e.c. = not elsewhere classified, NPISHs = nonprofit institutions serving households.

Note: The classification used is the same as the one used for the 2017 ICP and 2011 ICP revised results.

[a] Reference purchasing power parities, as listed in Appendix 2, were used.

[b] Only one set of items of construction inputs was used for each of the three basic headings of construction.

[c] Only one set of calculations was done by combining the two basic headings actual and imputed rental.

Sources: Economy sources; and World Bank. 2016b. *International Comparison Program: Classification of Final Expenditure on GDP*. Washington, DC: World Bank. http://pubdocs.worldbank.org/en/708531575560035925/pdf/ICP-Classification-description-2019-1205.pdf.

Appendix 4: List of Implementing Agencies and Local Currency Units Used

Economy	Implementing Agency	Local Currency Unit
Bangladesh	Bangladesh Bureau of Statistics	taka (Tk)
Bhutan	National Statistics Bureau	ngultrum (Nu)
Brunei Darussalam	Department of Economic Planning and Statistics	Brunei dollar (B$)
Cambodia	National Institute of Statistics	riel (KR)
Fiji	Fiji Bureau of Statistics	Fiji dollar (F$)
Hong Kong, China	Census and Statistics Department	Hong Kong dollar (HK$)
India	Ministry of Statistics and Programme Implementation	Indian rupee (₹)
Indonesia	Badan Pusat Statistik	rupiah (Rp)
Lao People's Democratic Republic	Lao Statistics Bureau	kip (KN)
Malaysia	Department of Statistics Malaysia	ringgit (RM)
Maldives	National Bureau of Statistics	rufiyaa (Rf)
Mongolia	National Statistical Office	togrog (MNT)
Nepal	Central Bureau of Statistics	Nepalese rupee (NRe/NRs)
Pakistan	Pakistan Bureau of Statistics	Pakistani rupee (PRe/PRs)
Philippines	Philippine Statistics Authority	peso (₱)
Singapore	Department of Statistics	Singapore dollar (S$)
Sri Lanka	Department of Census and Statistics	Sri Lankan rupee (SLRe/SLRs)
Taipei,China	Directorate-General of Budget, Accounting and Statistics	NT dollar (NT$)
Thailand	Trade Policy and Strategy Office	baht (B)
Viet Nam	General Statistics Office	dong (D)

Source: Asian Development Bank.

Glossary

Term	Definition
Acquisitions	Goods (including assets) and services acquired by institutional units when they become the new owners of the goods or when the delivery of services to them is completed.
Actual individual consumption by households (AICH)	The sum of individual consumption expenditures by households (ICEH), expenditures by nonprofit institutions serving households (NPISHs), and individual consumption expenditure by government (ICEG) at purchasers' prices.
Additivity	A concept that the expenditures for higher-level aggregates can be obtained simply by adding real expenditures of the subaggregates of which they are composed. Real expenditures obtained using Gini-Élteto-Köves-Szulc (GEKS)-based purchasing power parities (PPPs) are not additive, so the sum of the real expenditures for the components of gross domestic product (GDP) does not equal the real expenditure on GDP.
Aggregation	The process of weighting and averaging PPPs for basic headings to obtain PPPs for each level of aggregation up to GDP.
Base currency	The currency unit selected to be the common currency in which PPPs and real and nominal expenditures are expressed. The base currency is also called the "numeraire currency" or the "reference currency."
Base economy	The economy, or group of economies, for which the value of the PPP is set at 1.00 and the value of the price level index (PLI) and the volume index is set at 100. The base economy is also known as the "reference economy."
Base economy invariance, invariant	The property under which the relativities between any two economies' PPPs, PLIs, or volume indexes are not affected by the choice of reference economy.
Basic heading	In principle, a group of similar, well-defined goods or services for which a sample of products can be selected that is representative of both product type and the purchases made in economies. In practice, a basic heading is defined as the lowest-level aggregate for which expenditure data are available.
Benchmark	A standard, or point of reference, against which an estimate can be compared, assessed, measured, or judged. PPPs are calculated using price data from a full list of household and nonhousehold products and weights derived from the expenditures on GDP for a specified reference year. In the International Comparison Program (ICP), a reference year is often referred to as a "benchmark year" or simply a "benchmark."

Term	Definition
Big Mac index	An index developed and used by *The Economist* to illustrate the use of PPPs. It is based on a comparison of prices of a McDonald's Big Mac burger across different economies.
Binary comparison	A price or volume comparison between two economies that draws on data only for those two economies. Binary comparison is also referred to as "bilateral comparison."
Capital city	The urban center in the participating economy where the seat of government is located. It is usually a city with a large share of the economy's population, and so contributes a significant part of the economy's GDP.
Capital-to-national price adjustments	Coefficients used in scaling capital-city average prices to national average prices using information from the price data collected for a benchmark ICP cycle.
Changes in inventories	The value of physical changes in inventories of raw materials, supplies, and finished goods held by producers; inventories of goods acquired for resale by wholesalers and retailers; inventories of goods stored by government; work-in-progress in manufacturing, construction, and service industries; or work-in-progress on cultivated assets (e.g., the natural growth prior to harvest of agricultural crops, vineyards, orchards, plantations, and timber tracts, and the natural growth in livestock raised for slaughter).
Classification of individual consumption according to purpose (COICOP)	A classification used to identify the objectives of both individual consumption expenditure and actual individual consumption.
Collective consumption expenditure by government (CCEG)	The final consumption expenditure of government on collective services provided by the government to all members of the community simultaneously.
Comparability	A requirement for economies to price products that are identical or, if not identical, equivalent. Two or more products are said to be comparable either if their physical and economic characteristics are identical, or if they are sufficiently similar that consumers are indifferent to the choice between them.
Compensation of employees	The total remuneration, in cash or in kind, payable by enterprises to employees in return for their work during a given accounting period. In the context of the ICP, it refers to the compensation paid to government employees.
Component	A subset of goods or services (or both) that make up some defined aggregate.
Consumer price index (CPI)	An index of price changes in consumer goods and services within an economy across time.

Term	Definition
Core product list	The reduced list of products priced in 2016 and used in this study, derived as a subset of the 2011 ICP product list to represent the basic headings instead of the full list of items. For this research study, fast-evolving products (definition below) were added to the core list.
Core-to-full adjustment factors	Coefficients, based on relationships between the PPPs of the core list and the PPPs of the full list of items at the basic-heading level observed from the ICP's 2011 cycle, and used to adjust corresponding basic-heading level PPPs for 2016, calculated using the core product list to make them consistent with the full-list PPPs for each basic heading.
Country-product-dummy (CPD) method	A multilateral method used to obtain transitive PPPs at the basic-heading level through regression analysis. This method is anchored on the law of "one price," which simply states that the observed price of a commodity in an economy is the product of the international average price of the commodity, the general price level in the economy, and a random disturbance term. This method regresses the natural logarithm of price on economy and product dummy variables, hence the label. The method also produces measures of reliability for the estimated PPPs.
Durable goods	Goods that are not consumed in a single use and can be used for a period of time, usually 3 or more years.
Dwellings	Buildings that are used entirely or primarily as residences, including any associated structures, such as garages, and all permanent fixtures customarily installed in residences. Movable structures, such as caravans, used as principal residences of households are included.
Expenditure per capita	Total expenditure divided by the total population of a given economy or the referenced geographic area.
Expenditure weight or share	The share of nominal expenditure of a basic heading or expenditure share of a higher-level component of GDP.
Expenditure relatives	Real measures expressed in index form with the level of an individual economy or an average for a group (such as the Asia and Pacific region) set to a value of 100.
Fast-evolving products	Products that change in nature over short periods, such as frequent changes in models and specifications.
Final consumption	Goods and services used by individual households or the community to satisfy their individual or collective needs or wants.

Term	Definition
Full product list	In the context of this research study on 2016 data, the full product list is the complete list of products (household and nonhousehold) priced by participating economies in an ICP benchmark year.
Gini-Éltető-Köves-Szulc (GEKS) method	The GEKS method produces transitive PPPs that are as close as possible to the nontransitive PPPs originally calculated in the binary comparisons. This procedure is also called the Éltető-Koves-Szulc method.
Goods	Physical objects for which a demand exists, over which ownership rights can be established, and whose ownership can be transferred from one institutional unit to another by engaging in transactions on the market. They are in demand because they may be used to satisfy the needs or wants of households or the community, or used to produce other goods or services.
Government final consumption expenditure (GFCE)	The total value of actual and imputed final consumption expenditures incurred by government on individual goods and services and final consumption expenditure of government on collective services.
Gross capital formation (GCF)	The total value of expenditure on gross fixed capital formation (GFCF), changes in inventories, and acquisitions less disposals of valuables.
Gross domestic product (GDP)—expenditure based	Actual individual consumption by households (AICH) at purchasers' prices *plus* collective consumption expenditure by government (CCEG) at purchasers' prices *plus* gross capital formation (GCF) at purchasers' prices *plus* the free-on-board value of exports of goods and services less the free-on-board value of imports of goods and services.
Gross fixed capital formation (GFCF)	The total value of acquisitions less disposals of fixed assets by resident institutional units during a given accounting period *plus* the additions to the value of nonproduced assets realized by the productive activity of resident institutional units.
Individual consumption expenditure by government (ICEG)	The total value of actual and imputed final consumption expenditures incurred by government on behalf of individuals. These include expenditures incurred by the government considered to be individual services, such as housing, health, recreation and culture, education, and social protection.
Individual consumption expenditure by households (ICEH)	The total value of actual and imputed final consumption expenditures incurred by households for goods and services consumed by the households. In the context of this research study on 2016 data, ICEH also includes individual consumption expenditure by nonprofit institutions serving households (NPISHs).
Intereconomy data validation	The process in which the average prices for the same products in different economies are checked against each other.

Term	Definition
Intraeconomy data validation	The process in which the individual price observations are edited and checked for variations within economies. It is also the level of validation at which the first checks are carried out on the average prices of an economy.
Local currency unit (LCU)	The monetary unit in which economic values are expressed in an economy.
Lorenz curve	A graphical representation of the distribution of income or wealth developed by Max Lorenz in 1905. The horizontal axis of the graph represents the poorest to richest cumulative percentiles of population, while the vertical axis represents the cumulative income or wealth.
Multilateral comparison	A simultaneous price or volume comparison between all pairs of economies within a group of economies of interest.
National annual average price	A price that has been averaged over all price quotations and across all localities of an economy to account for regional variations in prices and over the days, weeks, months, or quarters of the reference calendar year to allow for seasonal variations in prices.
Net purchases abroad	Purchases by residential households in the rest of the world (as tourists, people traveling on business, government officials, crews, border and seasonal workers, diplomatic and military personnel stationed abroad) *less* purchases by nonresidential households in the economic territory of the economy (as tourists, people traveling on business, government officials, crews, border and seasonal workers, diplomatic and military personnel stationed abroad).
Nominal expenditure	Expenditure in the currency units of an economy, converted to a common currency using the exchange rate of a reference economy.
Nonprofit institutions serving households (NPISHs)	Nonprofit institutions that are not predominantly financed and controlled by government; that provide goods or services to households free or at prices that are not economically significant; and whose main resources are voluntary contributions by households.
Outlet	A shop, market, service establishment, internet site, mail order service, or other place from where goods or services can be purchased, and from where the purchasers' or list prices of the items sold can be obtained.
Outlier	A term generally used to describe any extreme value in a set of survey data. Extreme values are not necessarily wrong, but the fact that they are considered extreme suggests that they need to be investigated to establish whether they are actual errors.
Price	The price of a good or service defined as the value of one unit of that good or service.

Term	Definition
Price level index (PLI)	The ratio of PPP to exchange rate with respect to a common reference currency. PLI is expressed as an index and is measured relative to a reference economy or relative to a whole region whose PLI value is 100.
Productivity adjustment	An adjustment made to wages and salaries of employees in different economies to reflect differences in labor productivity across economies.
Purchasing power parity (PPP)	The number of currency units required in a given economy to purchase a common basket of goods and services, which can be purchased with one unit of the reference currency in the reference economy.
Real expenditure	Expenditure in local currency units converted into a common currency unit using purchasing power parities.
Reference purchasing power parities (PPPs)	Used for basic headings for which it is difficult to collect price data. PPPs of a closely related basic heading or a group of basic headings are used as reference PPPs.
Relative price levels	The ratios of PPPs for components of GDP relative to the overall PPP for GDP for an economy. Relative price levels indicate whether the price level for a given basic heading or aggregate is higher or lower relative to the general price level in the economy.
Rest of the world	Consists of all nonresident institutional units that enter into transactions with resident units, or that have other economic links with resident units.
Services	The result of a production activity that changes the conditions of the consuming units, or facilitates the exchange of products or financial assets.
Structured product descriptions (SPDs)	Generic descriptions that list price-determining characteristics relevant to a particular narrow cluster of products.
System of National Accounts (SNA)	A coherent, consistent, and integrated set of macroeconomic accounts, balance sheets, and tables based on a set of internationally agreed concepts, definitions, classifications, and accounting rules (United Nations 2009).
Transitivity	An important property of PPP, whereby the direct PPP between any two economies yields the same result as an indirect comparison via any other economy.
Volume measures	Another term for real expenditures.

References

S. Ahmad. 1980. Approaches to Purchasing Power Parity and Real Product Comparisons Using Shortcuts and Reduced Information. *World Bank Staff Working Paper Series*. No. 418. Washington, DC: World Bank.

Asian Development Bank (ADB). 2007. *2005 International Comparison Program in Asia and the Pacific: Purchasing Power Parities and Real Expenditures*. Manila: Asian Development Bank. https://www.adb.org/publications/purchasing-power-parities-and-real-expenditures-2007.

ADB. 2008. *Research Study on Poverty-Specific Purchasing Power Parities for Selected Countries in Asia and the Pacific*. Manila: Asian Development Bank. https://www.adb.org/sites/default/files/publication/29130/poverty-specific-ppp.pdf.

ADB. 2012a. *2009 Purchasing Power Parity Update for Selected Economies in Asia and the Pacific: A Research Study*. Manila: Asian Development Bank. https://www.adb.org/publications/2009-purchasing-power-parity-update-selected-economies-asia-and-pacific-research-study.

ADB. 2012b. *Supply and Use Tables for Selected Economies in Asia and the Pacific*. Manila: Asian Development Bank. https://www.adb.org/publications/supply-and-use-tables-selected-economies-asia-and-pacific-research-study.

ADB. 2014. *Purchasing Power Parities and Real Expenditures*. Manila: Asian Development Bank. https://www.adb.org/publications/purchasing-power-parities-and-real-expenditures.

ADB. 2017. *Compendium of Supply and Use Tables for Selected Economies in Asia and the Pacific*. Manila: Asian Development Bank. http://dx.doi.org/10.22617/TCS179096-2.

ADB. 2019. *Key Indicators for Asia and the Pacific 2019*. Manila: Asian Development Bank. https://dx.doi.org/10.22617/FLS190428-3.

ADB. 2020. *2017 International Comparison Program for Asia and the Pacific Purchasing Power Parities and Real Expenditures: Results and Methodology*. Manila: Asian Development Bank. http://dx.doi.org/10.22617/TCS200012-2.

C. Clague. 1986. Short-Cut Estimates of Real Income. *Review of Income and Wealth, International Association for Research in Income and Wealth*. 32 (3). pp. 313–331. https://doi.org/10.1111/j.1475-4991.1986.tb00542.x.

E. Dalgaard and H. S. Sørensen. 2002. *Consistency between PPP Benchmarks and National Price and Volume Indices*. Paper prepared for the 27th General Conference of the International Association for Research in Income and Wealth. Stockholm, Sweden. 18–24 August.

A. Deaton. 2012. *Calibrating Measurement Uncertainty in Purchasing Power Parity Exchange Rates*. Paper prepared for the 7th meeting of the 2011 International Comparison Program Technical Advisory Group. Washington, DC. 17–18 September. http://documents.worldbank.org/curated/en/147281468336658081/pdf/907230WP001-030t0Box0385325B0PUBLIC.pdf.

A. Deaton and B. Aten. 2017. Trying to Understand the PPPs in ICP 2011: Why Are the Results So Different? *American Economic Journal: Macroeconomics*. 9 (1). pp. 243–264. https://doi.org/10.1257/mac.20150153.

W.E. Diewert. 2013. Irving Fisher and Index Number Theory. *Journal of the History of Economic Thought*. 35 (2). pp. 199–232, https://doi.org/10.1017/S1053837213000072.

The Economist. 2020. Burgernomics: The Big Mac index. *The Economist Group.* 15 July. https://www.economist.com/big-mac-index.

R.C. Feenstra, R. Inklaar, and M. P. Timmer. 2015. The Next Generation of the Penn World Table. *American Economic Review.* 105 (10). pp. 3150–3182. https://www.aeaweb.org/articles?id=10.1257/aer.20130954.

M. Gilbert and associates. 1958. *Comparative National Products and Price Levels: A Study of Western Europe and the United States.* Paris: Organisation for European Economic Co-operation.

M. Gilbert and I. Kravis. 1954. *An International Comparison of National Products and Purchasing Power of Currencies: A Study of the United States, the United Kingdom, France, Germany, and Italy.* Paris: Organisation for European Economic Co-operation.

R.C. Inklaar. 2019. *Productivity Adjustment in ICP.* Paper presented at the Fourth International Comparison Program Technical Advisory Group Meeting. Washington, DC. 28–29 October.

R.C. Inklaar and D. S. P. Rao. 2017. Cross-Country Income Levels over Time: Did the Developing World Suddenly Become Much Richer? *American Economic Journal: Macroeconomics.* 9 (1). pp. 265–290. https://doi.org/10.1257/mac.20150155.

R.C. Inklaar and D. S. P. Rao. 2019. *Building PPP time series.* Paper presented at the Third International Comparison Program Technical Advisory Group Meeting and Fourth Task Force Meeting. Washington, DC. 2–3 May. http://pubdocs.worldbank.org/en/385611558463358273/pdf/ICP-TAG03-S24-PT-Building-PPP-time-series-Inklaar-and-Rao.pdf.

R.C. Inklaar and M. P. Timmer. 2013. A Note on Extrapolating PPPs. In *Measuring the Real Size of the World Economy*, edited by the World Bank. Washington, DC: World Bank.

International Monetary Fund. International Financial Statistics. https://data.imf.org/ (accessed 17 September 2019 and 21 January 2020).

I.B. Kravis, A. Heston, and R. Summers. 1978. Real GDP Per Capita for More Than One Hundred Countries. *The Economic Journal.* 88 (350). pp. 215–242. https://doi.org/10.2307/2232127.

I.B. Kravis and R. E. Lipsey. 1983. Toward an Explanation of National Price Levels. *Princeton Studies in International Finance.* 52. Princeton University, United States.

P. McCarthy. 2013. Extrapolating PPPs and Comparing ICP Benchmark Results. In *Measuring the Real Size of the World Economy*, edited by the World Bank. Washington, DC: World Bank.

D.S.P. Rao. 2013. The Framework of the International Comparison Program. In *Measuring the Real Size of the World Economy*, edited by the World Bank. Washington, DC: World Bank.

R. Summers and A. Heston. 1991. The Penn World Table (Mark 5): An Expanded Set of International Comparisons, 1950–1988. *The Quarterly Journal of Economics.* 106 (2). pp. 327–368. https://doi.org/10.2307/2937941.

United Nations. 2009. *System of National Accounts 2008.* New York: United Nations. https://unstats.un.org/unsd/nationalaccount/docs/SNA2008.pdf.

United Nations. 2015. *Resolution Adopted by the General Assembly on 25 September 2015.* Prepared for the 70th Session of the United Nations General Assembly. New York: United Nations.

United Nations Economic and Social Council (ECOSOC). 2016a. *Final Report of the Friends of the Chair Group on the Evaluation of the 2011 Round of the International Comparison Programme.* New York: United Nations.

United Nations Economic and Social Council (ECOSOC). 2016b. *Statistical Commission: Report of the Forty-Seventh Session.* 8–11 March. New York: United Nations.

S. Varjonen. 2002. *Improving the Quality of PPP Series*. Paris: Organisation for Economic Co-operation and Development. www.oecd.org/dataoecd/51/21/1961624.pdf.

World Bank. 2015. *Purchasing Power Parities and the Real Size of World Economies: A Comprehensive Report of the 2011 International Comparison Program*. Washington, DC: World Bank. https://doi.org/10.1596/978-1-4648-0329-1.

World Bank. 2016. *International Comparison Program: Classification of Final Expenditure on GDP*. Washington, DC: World Bank. http://pubdocs.worldbank.org/en/708531575560035925/pdf/ICP-Classification-description-2019-1205.pdf.

World Bank. 2020. *Purchasing Power Parities and the Size of World Economies: Results from the 2017 International Comparison Program*. Washington, DC: World Bank. https://doi.org/10.1596/978-1-4648-1530-0.

www.ingramcontent.com/pod-product-compliance
Lightning Source LLC
Chambersburg PA
CBHW050047220326
41599CB00045B/7315